The Life and Thought
of
KANZO UCHIMURA

The Life and Thought

of
KANZO UCHIMURA
1861-1930

HIROSHI MIURA

WILLIAM B. EERDMANS PUBLISHING COMPANY
GRAND RAPIDS, MICHIGAN / CAMBRIDGE, U.K.

© 1996 Hiroshi Miura

Published by Wm. B. Eerdmans Publishing Co.

255 Jefferson Ave. S.E., Grand Rapids, Michigan 49503 /

P.O. Box 163, Cambridge CB3 9PU U.K.

Printed in the United States of America

01 00 99 98 97   7 6 5 4 3 2 1

Library of Congress Cataloging-in-Publication Data

Miura, Hiroshi.

The life and thought of Kanzo Uchimura, 1861-1930 / Hiroshi Miura.

p.   cm.

Includes bibliographical references and index.

ISBN 0-8028-4205-4 (pbk. : alk. paper)

1. Uchimura, Kanzo, 1861-1930. 2. Christian biography — Japan.

I. Title.

BR1317.U25M58 1997

275.2'082'092 — dc21

[B]   96-52638

CIP

To the memory of my parents,
Yokichiro and Chikano Miura

Contents

Acknowledgments

This book is derived from a thesis that I submitted to the University of Aberdeen, Scotland. First of all, I wish to express my gratitude to Dr. Louise Kellogg, trustee emeritus at Alaska Pacific University, Anchorage, Alaska, for awarding me a scholarship which partially covered my research expenses while studying at the University of Aberdeen. I am also grateful to Dr. James Cox, former head of Value and Religious Studies at Alaska Pacific University, now a lecturer in the Centre for the Study of Christianity in the Non-Western World (CSCNWW), University of Edinburgh, and Dr. Robert Elting, former associate professor at Alaska Pacific University, for encouraging me in my studies. Special thanks go to Professor Andrew F. Walls, former head of the Department of Religious Studies, University of Aberdeen, who gave me constructive advice for the original manuscript. I also wish to express my thanks to Mr. J. Derrick McClure of the Department of English, University of Aberdeen, and Dr. Lynne Wheatley, for their guidance on the English language; Mr. McClure also undertook the demanding task of reading the proofs. Thanks must go to Dr. John Parratt, formerly of the University of Edinburgh, for his advice on the publication process. Finally, I would like to thank Mr. Masayuki Shima, a longtime friend, who loaned me valuable materials for my research on Kanzo Uchimura and the Mukyokai Christian Movement.

HIROSHI MIURA

CHAPTER 1

The Historical Background of Japan as a Setting for Uchimura's Life and Thoughts

1. The First European Contact with Japan and the Introduction of Christianity

The first Europeans to come to Japan, Portuguese traders, arrived in Kyushu, the main southern island of Japan, in 1542, and engaged in the trade of firearms with the local feudal lords. Christianity was introduced to Japan a few years later, between 1549 and 1551, by Jesuit missionaries led by Saint Francis Xavier (1506-52), a native Basque. Xavier and other Jesuits had considerable success, converting about one hundred fifty thousand Japanese to Christianity around 1580, and about three hundred thousand in 1614.[1] The percentage of people who were Christians in Japan at that time was higher than now, comprising not only the ordinary people but also some daimyos (feudal lords).

Why did so many Japanese become *Kirishitan*, as the Catholics of that period are called in Japanese? One scholar, Norihisa Suzuki, suspects that it was because Japan had just gone through two centuries of civil war, Sengoku-jidai (the Age of the Country at War), when Christianity

---

1. The ratio of Christians to non-Christians in Japan was about three times higher than it is today. Norihisa Suzuki, "Christianity," in *Japanese Religion — A Survey by the Agency for Cultural Affairs* (Tokyo: Kodansha International, 1981), pp. 76-77.

I

was first introduced. The old social order had fallen, and the surviving feudal lords were engaged in a struggle for power. In trying to adapt to this situation, men were seeking a new system of values that would provide them with some sense of meaning and enable them to live through those days. The traditional religions of Japan could not satisfy their needs.[2]

2. National Isolation (1587-1854)

In 1587 Hideyoshi Toyotomi, who ruled Japan from 1582 to 1598, suddenly issued an edict ordering the Jesuit missionaries to leave Japan and all Japanese Christians to give up their faith or face persecution. Hideyoshi's order was not enforced strictly, but it did make Christian life more difficult. In 1614 Ieyasu Tokugawa (1543-1616), first of the Tokugawas shoguns,[3] issued and enforced an edict aimed at extinguishing the Christian faith in Japan, and the succeeding shoguns maintained the ban. Hideyoshi and the Tokugawas who followed him had no particular objection to Christianity on religious grounds, but looked upon it with deep suspicion because they thought it was politically dangerous. They believed this considerable group of Japanese who had allegiance to the Pope in Europe could not be trusted and posed a possible threat to the reestablished unity of Japan. Furthermore, they were aware of the colonial expansion of European powers in Southeast Asia, where Christian missionaries seemed to serve as forerunners to military expeditions from their respective countries. The Japanese rulers wanted to keep trade relations with the Europeans, but they gradually came to the conclusion that, for reasons of national security and political stability, Christianity had to be eliminated. Thus, for nearly three centuries, until the Christian faith was once again permitted when Japan was forced to reopen its doors to the outside world in the mid–nineteenth century, Christianity was officially banned in Japan. Because of this and the severe punishment imposed on those who broke the ban, there was no very significant Christian movement in Japan during this period. Christians in these years, called *Kakure Kirishitan* (the Hidden

2. Suzuki, pp. 76-77.

3. In pre-Meiji times the actual ruler of Japan; succession was hereditary as long as a family could remain in power. The shogun was always invested by the emperor.

Christians), concealed their faith, camouflaging it with Shinto and Buddhist symbols in order to pass it from generation to generation.

3. The Tokugawa (Edo) Period (1603-1867)

The Tokugawa family ruled Japan from Edo (modern Tokyo). During the Tokugawa period, a policy called *sakoku* (national isolation) was instituted, which not only banned foreign missionaries but also prohibited all foreigners from entering Japan as well as Japanese from going abroad. Despite this isolation policy, the Tokugawas did permit some contact with the outside world. They preserved Nagasaki, a port town in Kyushu, as a window looking out on the rest of the world, which authorized Chinese and Dutch traders only were allowed to visit. The Tokugawa shogunate (military government) ruled Japan by supervising daimyos and dividing people into four classes — samurai,[4] farmers, artisans, and merchants, in descending order of status — drawing a sharp line between the samurai, the ruling class, and the rest of the people. This segregation system was based on the social theories of Confucianism, developed many years earlier in China.[5]

4. Confucianism in the Tokugawa Period

The early Tokugawas not only borrowed Confucianism's social theories but also encouraged the study of its philosophy. Confucianism seemed well suited to benefit the ruler because it emphasized the common people's loyalty to him. Razan Hayashi (1583-1657), an expert in Confucian ethics, became an adviser to the first three Tokugawa shoguns, and, as a result, a school of Confucianism was established at Edo. This scholarly interest also produced the development within the samurai class of a body of trained students and thinkers. The long period of interest in Confucianism also made Japanese people as a whole keep to high ethical and moral standards; Confucianism was also the source for Bu-

4. The warriors in feudal Japan. Characteristically they carried two swords at their side.
5. Edwin O. Reischauer, *Japan: Past and Present* (London: Gerald Duckworth, 1964), pp. 85-86.

shido,[6] the unwritten ethical code of the samurai. Although Buddhism was the state religion during this period, when it started to decline Confucianism became the dominant philosophy in Tokugawa Japan.

5. The Influence of Japan's Geographical Position on Its Culture

Japan is an island country located about five hundred miles from mainland China. She was neither conquered nor invaded by foreign forces until after the Second World War, although she has been culturally influenced by China since ancient times. Japan's geographical location played a critical role in forming Japanese culture. That is to say, the influence of foreign cultures brought slow changes, but was never overwhelming. In addition, the Tokugawa regime's nearly three-century-long policy of isolation helped Japan develop its own cultural identity. Thus Japan largely preserved a cultural tradition undiluted until modern times, unlike China.[7]

6. The End of Japan's Isolation

In the first half of the nineteenth century the Russians, British, and Americans frequently approached Japan with requests to begin trade. The Americans especially were interested because their whaling ships often operated in the North Pacific and wanted to visit Japanese ports to take on water and fresh food. The Edo government, however, stood firm on its old isolation policy. It was clear that the Tokugawa regime would not voluntarily open its doors to foreign countries, so the American government decided to force them open. For this purpose, it sent a naval fleet, under Commodore Matthew C. Perry, to Japan in July 1853. Perry delivered a letter from U.S. president Millard Fillmore to the shogun,

6. Inazo Nitobe itemized the following as Bushido: rectitude or justice, courage, benevolence, politeness, sincerity, honor, loyalty, and self-control. Inazo Nitobe, *Bushido: The Soul of Japan,* 17th ed. (Rutland, Vt.: Charles E. Tuttle, 1984).

7. Shigeru Matsumoto, introduction to *Japanese Religion — A Survey by the Agency for Cultural Affairs,* ed. Ichiro Hori, Fujio Ikado, Tsuneya Wakimoto, and Keiichi Yanagawa (Tokyo: Kodansha International, 1981), pp. 12-13.

demanding to start trade relations, thus throwing the Tokugawa government into sudden crisis. In the face of the enormous guns of the American warships, the Tokugawas realized that Japan's own shore batteries were almost useless. When Perry's fleet returned to Japan in February 1854, the Tokugawas had no choice but to sign a treaty with the United States, opening two ports to American vessels and permitting limited trade. In the following two years the government signed similar treaties with Britain, Russia, and Holland. Thus the period of national isolation, which had lasted nearly three centuries, ended. However, the Kyoto court, which included the emperor and the majority of the daimyos, opposed the Tokugawas' policy of opening up the country to foreigners. The cry of "expel the barbarians"[8] grew all over the country.

The end of the Tokugawa regime came in November 1867 when Shogun Yoshinobu Tokugawa voluntarily surrendered the rule of the country to the emperor. This event is called the *Meiji Restoration.*

7. The Meiji Period (1868-1912): The Time of Modernization

Although the emperor was the leader of the new government, he was not initially strong enough to head the government because he was only sixteen years old, so a group of young samurai from anti-Tokugawa clans, mainly from Satsuma[9] and Choshu,[10] gained control. Seeing how helpless their forces were against Western naval powers, the young samurai immediately abandoned their isolationist thinking and started to study the technology that made the West strong. They hoped to create a strong Japan that was not inferior to Western powers. Since they were military men, their thinking in modernizing Japan was naturally in terms of military strength. However, they knew that to achieve that goal, reforms in other areas such as the economy, politics, and education were necessary. Thus, modernization programs were rapidly started. The leaders were determined to learn the best from each Western country. For example, they sent students to Britain to study the navy and merchant marines,

8. The Japanese called foreigners "barbarians" at that time.
9. A feudal fief located in the southern end of Kyushu.
10. A clan located in the western tip of Honshu, the main island of Japan.

to Germany to study the army and medicine, to France for law, and to the United States for business.[11] The government also invited foreigners to advise Japanese schools as well as government organizations. Copying Western models, the Meiji government organized a prefectural system of rule; they formed a cabinet using Germany as a model, and drew up a constitution. They modernized the police force, the currency, and the postal system. They adopted the Western calendar but kept the old Chinese system of counting years by "year periods," beginning with the Meiji "year period." Each "year period" was identical in duration with the reign of an emperor.

The Constitution

Hirobumi Itoh (1841-1909), a former samurai from Choshu, was assigned to study the Western constitutions and to draft one for Japan. After visiting various European countries, he deemed the German constitution best suited to Japan's needs and, referring to it, drew up the Japanese Constitution in 1889. It clearly stated that the emperor was the head of the state.

Education

The Ministry of Education was formed in 1871, followed by a universal educational system that, within a few years, accepted almost all children of school age. Primary education with a minimum of three years' attendance became compulsory for everyone in 1880. Boys could go to middle schools for five years or to special technical schools. Girls could go to higher schools for four or five years. Furthermore, the boys' middle school led to various higher technical schools or to the men's higher school, which offered professional training as well as preparatory education for entrance to the imperial universities.

As Edwin O. Reischauer states, universal education enabled Japan to be the first Asian country to produce a literate population. The high rate of literacy among the population, as well as industrial strength and military power, explains why Japan played a dominant role in East Asia in the first

11. Reischauer, p. 123.

half of the twentieth century.[12] However, while Japan adopted Western technology, it also emphasized certain aspects of Japanese culture. Young Japanese were taught the glory of Japan's military tradition at school.

Economy

The government also took the initiative in setting up many industrial enterprises. It was directly involved with the railways, the telegraph system, the gas industry, shipbuilding, and mining. Government financial aid for new private enterprises such as the House of Mitsui and Iwasaki of Mitsubishi turned relatively small concerns into large economic empires, which were later called *zaibatsu*. Japan was in a unique position in the economic world. Using Western science and its own cheap labor — provided by the rural population — Japan attained massive low-cost production. One thing, however, should be noted. The ruling group was interested in developing a powerful nation rather than a prosperous people.[13]

Generally speaking, the forty-five years of the Meiji period were a time when the Japanese studied and adopted advanced Western civilization, and gradually assimilated it.

8. Japan's Renewed Contact with Christianity

When Japan opened its doors to the outside world in the mid–nineteenth century, Christianity was once again brought into the country, being tolerated in 1873. Catholic, Protestant, and Orthodox missionaries all arrived in Japan at about the same time. The Protestant Episcopal Church, the Presbyterian Church, and the Dutch Reformed Church were among the first Protestants to arrive from the United States. J. C. Hepburn, M.D., of the American Presbyterian Board of Foreign Missions, and Rev. Samuel R. Brown and Guido F. Verbeck, of the Dutch Reformed Church in America, arrived in 1859, Jonathan Goble in 1860, and James H. Ballagh in 1881. All were engaged in missionary work.

12. Reischauer, p. 128.
13. Reischauer, pp. 132-33.

The first modern missionaries included not only ministers but medical doctors as well.[14]

9. Protestant Christianity in Meiji Japan

In the early Meiji times, Protestant Christianity was spread to the country from three main centers: Yokohama, a port town south of Tokyo; Kumamoto in Kyushu; and Sapporo in Hokkaido.

The Yokohama Band

Samuel Brown opened a school for boys in Yokohama in the early 1870s, where English, general subjects, and theology were taught. This project helped convert people to Christianity. Under the supervision of Ballagh, also sent by the Dutch Reformed Church in America, the Nihon Kirisuto Kokai (the Church of Christ in Japan), the first Protestant church in Japan, was formed in Yokohama in 1872. This group of Christians, later called the Yokohama Band, produced Meiji-period Christian leaders such as Masahisa Uemura (1858-1925), Yoichi Honda, Kaiseki Matsumura, and Kajinosuke Ibuka.

The Kumamoto Band

In 1871 Captain Leroy L. Janes, a graduate of West Point and a retired officer of the United States Army, was invited by the daimyo of the area to teach English at a school in Kumamoto. Therefore, his connection with the school in the beginning had nothing to do with Christianity. A few years later, however, he offered to teach his students about the Bible in his own house, and in 1876 a number of them pledged to follow Christ and "to enlighten the darkness of the Empire by preaching the Gospel, even to the extent of sacrificing their lives."[15] When their conversion became

14. Stuart D. B. Picken, *Christianity and Japan* (Tokyo: Kodansha International, 1983), p. 52.

15. Otis Cary, *A History of Christianity in Japan* (Rutland, Vt.: Charles E. Tuttle, 1982), 2:123.

public, however, much pressure was placed on them. The authorities did not renew Janes's contract and the school was closed. Before Janes left Japan, however, he introduced his students to Jo Niijima (1843-90), the founder of Doshisha (now Doshisha University) in Kyoto, and the students went to Kyoto to study. This group produced Hiromichi Kozaki, who later became president of Doshisha; Danjo Ebina, a theologian; and Tsurin Kanamori, an evangelist. The Congregational Church (called *Kumiai Kyokai* in Japanese), which became the largest Protestant denomination in the Meiji period, was mainly supported by this group of Christians, the Kumamoto Band.

The Sapporo Band

The Sapporo Band of Christians gathered under the guidance of William S. Clark, president of the Massachusetts Agricultural College, who, at the invitation of the Japanese government, went to Sapporo in 1876 to help establish an agricultural college. From the beginning he tried, by word and deed, to be a good Christian example to the students. He stayed in Hokkaido less than a year, but within that short time every one of his fifteen students had agreed to Christian baptism. After Clark had left, these earnest students went on to persuade the class of the following year to sign the "Covenant of Believers in Jesus" that Clark had prepared. From this group, the Sapporo Band, people like Kanzo Uchimura and Inazo Nitobe (1862-1933) emerged.

Christianity as an organized religion did not spread quickly in modern Japan. However, the influence of Christianity on Japanese society is far greater than one might think from the percentage of Christians in the population, and has been especially strong in educational fields.

10. Building Up a Modern Military Power and an Empire

During the latter half of the nineteenth century, the European powers continued to build up their colonial empires by expanding their territories in Africa, Asia, and Oceania. Overseas expansion and colonial possessions were signs of a successful government at that time. Japanese leaders copied their European counterparts in obtaining territories abroad and extended their expansion program to the neighboring countries, namely, China and Korea, which were in political decline and militarily weak.

11. The Sino-Japanese War: 1894-95

In August 1894 the Japanese government declared war on China over Korea. Japan seized Korea without much difficulty, defeated the Chinese naval forces, and captured Wei-hai-wei on the Chinese mainland in a war that lasted nine months. The peace treaty in 1895 allowed Japan to obtain the Liaotung Peninsula and the island of Formosa (Taiwan) from China. By winning the war Japan had proved that she had considerable power.

12. Progression toward the Russo-Japanese War

Some European powers regarded the emergence of Japan as new competition to their territorial expansion programs. In 1895 Russia, Germany, and France, by mutual agreement, forced Japan to return the Liaotung Peninsula to China on the pretext that Japan's occupation of it disturbed the peace of East Asia. In 1898, however, these powers took their own pieces of land from China. France took Kwangchow Bay and the nearby islands in South China, Germany took Tsingtao and Kiaochow Bay, and Russia leased Port Arthur on the Liaotung Peninsula, which she had forced Japan to give up three years earlier. Britain also convinced the Chinese to grant her a leasehold on Wei-hai-wei in the north, and secured a ninety-nine-year lease on the Kowloon Peninsula in the south. Because of the presence of these Western powers in East Asia, Japan realized that she ought to form an alliance with one of them before she expanded her sphere of influence in Asia. In addition, she realized that Russia's military action in Manchuria and interference in Korea were the main problems to be overcome. The British also thought it a good idea to form an alliance with Japan in order to cope with the situation in East Asia. Thus, the Anglo-Japanese Alliance was signed in 1902. Japan therefore became an ally of Great Britain, the greatest empire and strongest naval power in the world of that day. Under the agreement, if one party made war with a third power, the other party would come to the aid of its ally.

13. The Russo-Japanese War: 1904-5

In February 1904 the Japanese naval fleet struck the units of the Russian naval forces at Port Arthur, then formally declared war. Russia was far stronger than Japan at that time, but had the disadvantage of fighting the war from several thousand miles away, at the end of the Trans-Siberian Railroad. Russia's war efforts were also obstructed by revolutionary movements back home. The Japanese consistently won battles in the Liaotung Peninsula ports and in Manchuria. And when the Russians sent their fleet from the Baltic Sea to East Asia, the entire Japanese navy attacked it in the Tsushima Straits, the channel between Japan and Korea, and destroyed it. Although Japan was victorious, she was on the verge of financial breakdown and was short of manpower, so she welcomed the peace arranged by the U.S. president, Theodore Roosevelt, in 1905. The conditions of the peace treaty were: (1) recognition of Japan's dominant political, military, and economic interests in Korea; (2) transfer to Japan of Russian rights in the Liaotung Peninsula and the southern section of the Manchurian Railway; and (3) cession to Japan of the southern half of Russia's Sakhalin Island, located north of Hokkaido. By defeating Russia, one of the major European powers, Japan herself had become one of the major powers in the world.

14. The Appearance of Modern Indigenous Culture

Toward the end of the Meiji period, modern and yet indigenous culture appeared. The literary world was naturally influenced by the West, but did not simply imitate Western literature. A Japanese style appeared. The works of novelist Soseki Natsume (1876-1916), for instance, were great literature, worthy of placement alongside the highest rated works of the Western world.[16] Yukichi Fukuzawa (1835-1901) was another example. A young samurai and student of Dutch in the late years of the Tokugawa period, Fukuzawa became a productive writer in Meiji times. He started a newspaper, *Jiji Shimpo,* and founded an educational institution, which became Keio University, in Tokyo. These people did not think of everything in terms of military strength, as the Satsuma and Choshu samurai had. It was clear that a new form of intellectual was growing up, and a new culture was appearing.

16. Reischauer, p. 144.

15. The First World War: 1914-17

In June 1914 the First World War broke out in Europe. Japan, an ally of Britain, immediately declared war on Germany and Austria. Unlike the war against Russia a decade earlier, the First World War was not a defensive war for Japan. Although no Japanese troops fought on European soil, in the East Japanese forces captured the German fortress of Tsingtao, and Japanese naval forces occupied the German-controlled Marshall, Mariana, and Caroline island groups in the Pacific Ocean. War in Europe gave Japan enormous economic prosperity. Japan supplied the needs not only of its own allies in Europe but also of China and India, because European supplies of goods to these Asian countries were stopped when the war in Europe advanced. The production of manufactured goods in Japan increased tremendously. Almost overnight, Japan became a creditor country instead of a debtor country.

16. The Taisho Period (1912-26):
The Appearance of Liberal Democratic Trends

The Meiji emperor died in 1912, leaving the throne to his son, who ruled the country using the reign title of Taisho. Hirobumi Itoh, who drafted the constitution and was four times prime minister, had been assassinated by a Korean in 1909. Aritomo Yamagata (1838-1922), founder of the army and twice prime minister, died in 1922. The death of these leading figures meant change. The economic prosperity that resulted from the First World War also indirectly helped popularize democratic ideals. With jobs plentiful and with no fear of losing work because of free expression, young people started to assert themselves both in word and action. Another factor that spurred democratic trends was the victory of the Western democratic countries in the First World War, which helped convince the ordinary Japanese that they fought against tyranny and militarism. The Russian Revolution in 1917 also furthered the democratic trend. In fact, democracy became central in discussions on government and politics.[17]

Such trends in Japanese society influenced the government. In 1922 Japan withdrew its troops from Vladivostok, Siberia. In the winter of

17. Reischauer, pp. 149-50.

1921-22 at the Washington Conference, Japan, together with the United States and other major European powers, agreed to reduce naval forces. In addition, the Japanese government reduced their four army divisions in 1925. It was also during this time that socialism came into being, and the Japan Socialists' Union was founded. Labor unions were formed among workers, and strikes became an everyday occurrence in the 1920s.

17. Nationalistic and Militaristic Reaction

The nationalistic and militaristic reaction of the 1930s was partly based on the remains of Japan's feudal past that had survived the modernization period of the late nineteenth and early twentieth century, says Reischauer.[18] Its spiritual source was the traditional Japanese idea of encouraging one's devotion to the nation. Also, it could be said that Japan's hundreds of years of rule by samurai made people ready to accept military leadership. People expected to be led.[19]

The Japanese army officers came from rural or small-town backgrounds, while their enlisted men were mostly from the poor peasant class. In the 1920s, the liberal philosophy of the city intellectuals and economic domination by big businesses were not acceptable in the eyes of these people, while so many unprivileged people, like the peasants, existed in Japan. They felt national reconstruction was needed. Such trends against liberalism and democracy grew, and were also influenced by occurrences outside Japan. The outside factors at this time were: (1) The fascist, totalitarian regimes that were gaining power in Europe, such as in Germany and Italy, impressed many Japanese with their "superiority." (2) Worldwide depression started, and in 1929 led to an international trade collapse. Large countries like Russia, the United States, and the British empire had their own natural resources and consuming markets, but Japan, a small country, depended entirely on other countries for both. Thus, for Japan, gaining natural resources and foreign market for export was vital. In addition, Japan's population increased to 60 million, which a simple agricultural economy could not support. Thus, seeking natural resources and foreign markets, Japan again started her colonial expansion.

18. Reischauer, p. 162.
19. Reischauer, p. 161.

The turning point of this liberal period came in September 1931, when Japanese army units stationed in Manchuria, northern China, started a war without the approval or even knowledge of the Tokyo government. They acted on the pretext of a story that Chinese troops had tried to blow up the Japanese-owned Manchurian Railway and, in a few months, had seized Manchuria, setting up a puppet government in January 1932. Soon after, Japanese naval forces landed at Shanghai in central China. The League of Nations and the United States condemned Japan's military action, but Japan did not change her attitude. Instead, she withdrew from the League of Nations in 1933. Thus Japan entered the so-called Fifteen-Years War,[20] which ended with Japan's defeat at the end of the Second World War, in 1945.

20. From the Manchurian Incident, which the Japanese army started in China in September 1931, to the conclusion of the Second World War, and Japan's defeat, in August 1945.

CHAPTER 2

The Life of Kanzo Uchimura

1. Birth to Fifteen Years Old

Kanzo Uchimura was born to Yoshiyuki and Yaso Uchimura on 23 March 1861, seven years before the Meiji Restoration and eight years after U.S. Commodore Matthew Perry's first visit to Edo (Tokyo) Bay. Yoshiyuki was a low-ranking samurai of the Takasaki clan. Under the Tokugawa feudal system, each clan had its own estate in Edo (Tokyo), the capital, which was where Kanzo was born. When Kanzo was seven years old, Yoshiyuki was ordered to return to Takasaki, the clan's center, about eighty miles northwest of Edo, and this is where Kanzo spent his childhood. In 1868, as a result of the Meiji Restoration, the Tokugawa shogunate fell, and at the same time the samurai system ended. Consequently, Yoshiyuki lost his position as a samurai with the Takasaki clan.

Kanzo's father was a devoted Confucian, and therefore Kanzo's early education was based on this system. In later years, Uchimura wrote a book entitled *How I Became a Christian: Out of My Diary,* which was in fact his autobiography. In this book he describes the moral education he received in his early childhood as follows:

> The story of a filial youth responding to an unreasonable demand of an old parent to have a tender bamboo-shoot (the asparagus of the Orient) at midwinter, of his search for it in [*sic*] forest, and of its miraculous sprout from under the snow is vivid to the memory of every child in my land as the story of Joseph to that of every Christian youth. Even parental tyranny and oppression were to be meekly borne, and

many illustrations were cited from the deeds of ancient worthies in this respect. Loyality [sic] to feudal lords, especially in time of war, took more romantic shapes in the ethical conceptions of the youth of my land. He was to consider his life as light as dust when called to serve his lord in exigency; and the noblest spot where he could die was in front of his master's steed, thrice blessed if his corpse was trampled under its hoof. — No less weightier [sic] was to be the youth's consideration for his master (his intellectual and moral preceptor), who was to him no mere school-teacher or college professor or quid pro quo principle [sic], but a veritable didaskalos, in whom he could and must completely confide the care of his body and soul. The Lord, the Father, and the Master, constituted his Trinity. Neither one of them was inferior to any other in his consideration.[1]

Yoshiyuki earnestly wanted his son to have a good education on the Western model, possibly because he thought the world was changing and his son needed good education to attain a good position in Japanese society. He therefore sent Kanzo to Arima School in Tokyo, a private educational institution, when he was twelve. Then, the following year, Kanzo entered Tokyo Gaikokugo Gakko (the Tokyo School of Foreign Language). Kanzo seems to have had a strong and sensitive religious susceptibility from his early childhood, because the following paragraph appears in his autobiography:

Every morning as soon as I washed myself, I offered this common prayer to each of the four groups of gods located in the four points of the compass, paying special attention to the eastern group, as the Rising Sun was the greatest of all gods. Where several temples were contiguous to one another, the trouble of repeating the same prayer so many times was very great; and I would often prefer a longer route with less [sic] number of sanctuaries in order to avoid the trouble of saying my prayers without scruples of my conscience.[2]

The religions in Japan at this time were mainly Buddhism, Shinto, and folk religion, and the gods Uchimura describes above were of the latter. Not until Kanzo was twelve years old was Christian faith permitted in

1. Kanzo Uchimura, *How I Became a Christian: Out of My Diary,* in *Uchimura Kanzo Zenshu* (The complete works of Kanzo Uchimura), 40 vols. (Tokyo: Iwanami Shoten, 1980-84), 3:10 (hereafter referred to as *Works*).

2. Uchimura, *How I Became a Christian,* p. 13.

Japan. In 1873, for the first time in over 250 years, the new Japanese government tolerated Christianity.

2. Sapporo Agricultural College and Encounter with Christianity

In 1876 Kanzo, at the age of sixteen, entered the Sapporo Agricultural College (SAC) in Sapporo, Hokkaido, the main northern island of Japan. At that time Hokkaido was a vast wilderness area. The new Japanese government planned to develop the island by founding an agricultural college in Sapporo to train talented men for this purpose. Because the national isolation of over two hundred years had put Japan in the 1870s far behind the United States and European countries in technology and industrial development, the Japanese government had to invite American advisers to the newly founded agricultural college. As it turned out, one of these American advisers brought the Christian religion into the college and the area for the first time, and Sapporo became one of three beachheads for Protestant Christianity in Japan. Subsequently, Kanzo was converted to Christianity, and this had an important influence on his entire life.

The Japanese government instructed the Japanese consul in Washington, D.C., Kiyonari Yoshida, to search for an appropriate adviser to SAC. Yoshida recommended William S. Clark, president of Massachusetts Agricultural College in Amherst. At that time New England was the most advanced area in the United States, and Massachusetts Agricultural College was one of the best schools of agriculture. Clark agreed to go to Sapporo for only one year while retaining his presidency in Amherst. In 1876 he sailed from the United States to Yokohama with his two assistants, Wheeler and Penhallow, with the understanding that they would stay after Clark had returned to the United States. A few months later, in July 1876, Clark set sail for Hokkaido. On the ship was a Japanese government official, Kiyotaka Kuroda, who was in charge of the newly founded agricultural college in Sapporo. An argument broke out on board between Clark and Kuroda about students' moral education in Sapporo. Clark was married to the daughter of a Congregational missionary and had an eager ambition to propagate the Christian gospel to the Japanese as a lay missionary.[3] For this reason, he had bought thirty English Bibles in

3. John F. Howes, "The Man Kanzo Uchimura," *Japan Studies*, no. 13 (spring 1968): 10.

Yokohama and carried them in his trunk for use in the classroom at Sapporo. Kuroda strongly opposed Clark's plan: Japan had Confucianism and Shinto, he said, therefore she did not need a foreign religion. Clark would be allowed to teach morals, but not Christianity. But Clark did not yield to Kuroda, and at last threatened to return to the United States if he could not carry out Christian education in Sapporo.[4] Kuroda was at a loss for an answer. This matter was not settled even after they arrived at Sapporo. However, shortly before the opening of the school, Kuroda gave in to Clark, telling him, "I will leave students' moral training to you. However, this is a government school. Therefore, treat the Bible as one of the literary works or a moral book."[5]

Clark stayed in Sapporo for only eight months. In spite of his short stay, his influence on the students was great. Although the official Japanese government document shows his title as assistant director and professor of agriculture and chemistry, he was, in effect, president of the institution. And under his influence, all his first-year students became Christians.

Kanzo entered SAC because the school offered free tuition and provided accommodation; moreover, the students were paid a monthly stipend by the Japanese government. Since Kanzo's family was so poor, these favorable terms were very attractive. Kanzo entered the college in the second year and studied primarily fishery science. By that time Clark had already gone back to America. However, those senior class students converted junior class students, such as Kanzo, to Christianity. Kanzo wrote in his autobiography that his conversion in the beginning was a forced one, and that he became a Christian against his own will. When the junior students were forced to convert to Christianity by senior students, Kanzo was the leader in resisting them. Kanzo's description of the circumstances is seen in his autobiography:

> One afternoon I resorted to a heathen temple in the vicinity, said to have been authorized by the Government to be the guardian-god of the district. At some distance from the sacred mirror which represented the invisible presence of the deity, I prostrated myself upon coarse dried grass, and there burst into a prayer as sincere and genuine as any I have ever offered to my Christian God since then. I beseeched that guard-

4. Hitoshi Masaike, *Uchimura Kanzo Den* (The life of Kanzo Uchimura) (Tokyo: Kyobunkan, 1977), p. 37.
5. Masaike, p. 37.

ian-god to speedily extinguish the new enthusiasm in my college, to punish such as those who obstinately refused to disown the strange god, and to help me in my humble endeavor in the patriotic cause I was upholding then. After the devotion I returned to my dormitory, again to be tormented with the most unwelcome persuasion to accept the few [*sic*] faith. The public opinion of the college was too strong against me, which it was beyond my power to withstand. They forced me to sign the covenant given below, somewhat in a manner of extreme temperance men prevailing upon an incorrigible drunkard to sign a temperance pledge. I finally yielded and signed it. I often ask myself whether I ought to have refrained from submitting myself to such a coercion. I was but a mere lad of sixteen then, and the boys who thus forced me "to come in" were all much bigger than I. So, you see, my first step toward Christianity was a forced one, against my will, and I must confess, somewhat against my conscience too.[6]

The "covenant" Kanzo mentions above was the "Covenant of Believers in Jesus" framed by Clark. Clark himself had signed it, as had those who decided to become Christians. The entire document is presented below.

Covenant of Believers in Jesus

The undersigned member of S.A. College, desiring to confess Christ according to his command, and to perform with true fidelity every Christian duty in order to show our love and gratitude to that blessed Savior who has made atonement for our sins by his death on the cross; and earnestly wishing to advance his Kingdom among men for the promotion of his glory and the salvation of those for whom he died, do solemnly covenant with God and with each other from this time forth to be his faithful disciples, and to live in strict compliance with the letter and the spirit of his teachings; and whenever a suitable opportunity offers we promise to present ourselves for examination, baptism and admission to some evangelical church.

"We believe the Bible to be the only direct revelation in language from God to man, and the only perfect and infallible guide to a glorious future life.

"We believe in one everlasting God who is our Merciful Father, our just and sovereign Ruler, and who is to be our final Judge.

---

6. Uchimura, *How I Became a Christian*, pp. 14-15.

"We believe that all who sincerely repent and by faith in the Son of God obtain the forgiveness of their sins, will be graciously guided through this life by the Holy Spirit and protected by the watchful providence of the Heavenly Father, and so at length prepared for the enjoyments and pursuits of the redeemed and holy ones; but that all who refuse to accept the invitation of the Gospel must perish in their sins, and be forever punished from the presence of the Lord.

"The following commandments we promise to remember and obey through all the vicissitudes of our earthly lives.

"Thou shalt love the Lord thy God with all thy heart and with all thy soul, and with all thy strength and with all thy mind; and thy neighbor as thyself.

"Thou shalt not worship any graven image or any likeness of any created being or thing.

"Thou shalt not take the name of the Lord thy God in vain.

"Remember the Sabbath day to keep it holy, avoiding all unnecessary labor, and devoting it as far as possible to the study of the Bible and the preparation of thyself and others for a holy life.

"Thou shalt obey and honor thy parents and rulers.

"Thou shalt not commit murder, adultery, or other impurity, theft or deception.

"Thou shalt do no evil to thy neighbor.

"Pray without ceasing."

For mutual assistance and encouragement we hereby constitute ourselves an association under the name "Believers in Jesus," and we promise faithfully to attend one or more meetings each week while living together, for the reading of the Bible or other religious books or papers, for conference and for social prayer; and we sincerely desire the manifest presence in our hearts of the Holy Spirit to quicken our love, to strengthen our faith, and to guide us into a saving knowledge of the truth.

S. — March 5, 1877[7]

Kanzo strongly resisted converting to Christianity. Once he converted, however, he was glad to have done so.

The practical advantage of the new faith was evident to me at once. — I was taught that there was but one God in the Universe, and not many,

---

7. Uchimura, *How I Became a Christian*, pp. 15-16.

— over eight millions — as I had formerly believed. The Christian monotheism laid its axe at the root of all my superstitions. All the vows I had made, and the manifold forms of worship with which I had been attempting to appease my angry gods, could now be dispensed with by owning this one God; and my reason and conscience responded "Yea!" One God, and not many, was indeed a glad tiding to my little soul. — I was not sorry that I was forced to sign the covenant of the "Believers in Jesus." Monotheism made me a new man.[8]

Kanzo and twelve other junior class students signed the "Covenant of Believers in Jesus" on 11 December 1877. In June of the following year seven of them, including Kanzo, were baptized by an American Methodist Episcopal missionary, Merriam Colbert Harris. At that time they thought they should adopt Christian names. So they looked into Webster's dictionary, and each selected a name. Kanzo named himself Jonathan, because he was "a strong advocate of the virtue of friendship, and Jonathan's love for David pleased him well."[9] Kanzo had two specially close friends in his class — Kingo Miyabe and Inazo Ohta (later his surname was changed to Nitobe) — and their friendship lasted throughout their lives. Miyabe later became a well-known botanist, and Nitobe an educationist who at one time served as under secretary-general at the League of Nations. Kanzo and the others who had received baptism from M. C. Harris joined the Methodist church because they knew he was a good man and thought that "his church must be good too."[10]

3. The Church in the Dormitory Room

Kanzo and his six Christian classmates started their own regular Christian meetings in their dormitory room. According to Uchimura's autobiography, the state of their Christian meeting was as follows:

> Our Sunday services were conducted on this wise: The little church was entirely democratic, and every one of us stood on the same ecclesiastical footing as the rest of the members. This we found to be thoroughly

8. Uchimura, *How I Became a Christian*, pp. 17-18.
9. Uchimura, *How I Became a Christian*, p. 20.
10. Uchimura, *How I Became a Christian*, pp. 17-18.

Biblical and Apostolic. The leadership of the meeting therefore devolved upon each one of us in turn. He was to be our pastor, priest, and teacher, — even servant — for the day. He was responsible for calling us together at the appointed time, his room was to be our church, and he must look [sic] how we were to be seated there. He alone could sit upon a stool, and his people sat before him in the true Oriental fashion, upon blankets spread upon the floor. For our pulpit, the mechanical Hugh [a practical member of the church] fitted up a flour-barrel which we covered with a blue-blanket. Thus dignified, the pastor opened the service with a prayer, which was followed by reading from the Bible. He then gave a little talk of his own, and called up each of his sheep to give a talk of his own in turn.[11]

The first-year and the second-year students had separate Christian meetings, but on Sunday evenings both groups came together to study the Bible. At that time, no Christian books were available in Japanese, so they relied mainly on English and American publications for their needs. The Religious Tract Society of London and the Society for Promoting Christian Knowledge sent them about one hundred volumes, and they had about eighty volumes from the American Tract Society, as well as bound volumes of *Illustrated Christian Weeklies*. At about this time, thinking they should prepare themselves for the circumstances they would encounter when they went out into the world, they tried an experiment at their Christian meeting: staging a debate between Christians and unbelievers. They divided their group into two sides, one representing the Christian and the other the unbeliever. The unbelieving side asked the Christians questions, which the Christian side then answered. The subject at their first meeting was "The Existence of God."

In July 1880 the senior class graduated from the college and laid plans to establish their own house of worship. They first approached the Reverend Mr. Denning, an Anglican missionary, for financial aid, because students in the senior class who had been baptized were attending services at an Anglican church in Sapporo. Denning gave them a negative answer. He thought another church was unnecessary because the Anglican mission already had a meeting place in Sapporo. By contrast, Rev. J. C. Davison,[12]

11. Uchimura, *How I Became a Christian*, p. 24.

12. By this time M. C. Harris, the Methodist missionary who administered baptism to Kanzo and others, had been replaced by Rev. J. C. Davison, who was stationed in Hakodate, southern Hokkaido.

a Methodist Episcopal missionary, offered four hundred U.S. dollars to help them build a church in Sapporo. Hitoshi Masaike, the author of *Uchimura Kanzo Den* (The life of Kanzo Uchimura), considers this offer a countermeasure against the Anglican church to establish a Methodist church in town.[13] At that time several Christian graduates from SAC were living together in a large house on a farm far from town. They were graduates from the same college, and had similar ideas. Therefore, they concluded that they should not be divided because some of them belonged to the Anglican church while others belonged to the Methodist church, and they rejected the idea of building a denominational church, such as a Methodist church, with financial aid from the Methodist mission. Here there was a difference of opinion between the Sapporo Christians and Davison; one side seeking an independent house of worship, the other offering to help build a Methodist church. The Sapporo Christians, therefore, borrowed the money, rather than taking it as a gift. They planned to return it as soon as possible. Kanzo wrote in his diary, "We felt for the first time in our Christian experience the evils of denominationalism."[14] In any case, on 24 March 1881 a four-hundred-dollar money order from Davison arrived. At this early stage, they planned to build a new building for their house of worship and called a carpenter to give them an estimate. However, they had difficulty obtaining a lot for the building, so they started searching for a structure that was already built.

Kanzo graduated 9 July 1881. His class had entered the college numbering twenty-one, but illness and dropouts had reduced that number to twelve at graduation. Graduating first in his class, Kanzo was granted the honor of giving an oration representing his class. Six other graduates were granted the opportunity to give graduation addresses as well. The names and the subjects were as follows:

"How Blessed Is Rest after Toil" — Mototaro Adachi
"The Importance of Morality to the Farmer" — Isamu Hiroi
"Agriculture as an Aid to Civilization" — Inazo Ohta (Nitobe)
"The Relation of Botany to Agriculture" — Kingo Miyabe
"The Relation of Chemistry to Agriculture" — Tamataro Takagi
"Fishery as a Science" — Kanzo Uchimura

13. Masaike, p. 57.
14. Uchimura, *How I Became a Christian*, p. 40.

From the beginning, Sapporo Agricultural College was founded to educate men of ability to develop Hokkaido. Graduates of the college were therefore given positions with the Japanese government and were expected to remain and work in Hokkaido. Because he had specialized in fishery science, Kanzo was given a position watching over fisheries on the island. His monthly salary was thirty yen, equivalent to thirty U.S. dollars then. Before taking up his job, however, Kanzo made a trip to Tokyo with his six Christian classmates. During this trip they visited many churches, exchanging information and trying to learn how to run a church, since they were to have one in Sapporo shortly. Kanzo wrote the following impression of his visit to metropolitan area churches.

> Though coming from the far north, from amidst primeval forests and bears and wolves, we found we were not the least intelligent among Christians. What we heard from the flour-barrel pulpit and talked about upon the blue blankets, were not the crudest thoughts when compared with the teachings and cultures of the metropolitan churches. On some points, indeed, we thought we had profounder and healthier views than our friends who were nurtured under the care of professional theologians.[15]

Kanzo also visited his family in Tokyo and did missionary work among them. Of all his family, his father seems to have been the most obstinately anti-Christian. Kanzo wrote in his autobiography:

> For three years I had been sending him books and pamphlets, and had written him constantly, imploring him to come to Christ and receive His salvation. He was a voracious reader and my books were not entirely ignored. But nothing could move him. He was a righteous man as far as social morality was concerned, and as is always the case with such a man, he was not one who felt the need of salvation most.[16]

At the end of his college course, he was awarded a little sum of money for his study. With this money, he bought five volumes of the *Commentary on the Gospel of St. Mark* by Faber, a German missionary in China. It was written in unpointed Chinese, and he thought that it might rouse his

15. Uchimura, *How I Became a Christian*, p. 51.
16. Uchimura, *How I Became a Christian*, p. 51.

father's intellectual appetite as a Confucian scholar to peruse it. Kanzo carried the volumes with him to his father.

> But alas! When I gave it to my father, no words of thanks or appreciation came from his lips, and all the best wishes of my heart met his coldest reception. I went into a closet and wept. The books were thrown into a box with other rubbish; but I took out the first volume and left it on his table. In his leisure when he had nothing else to do, he would read a page or so, and again it went into the rubbish. I took it out again, and placed it upon his table as before. My patience was as great as his reluctance to read these books. Finally, however, I prevailed; he went through the first volume! He stopped [scoffing] at Christianity! Something in the book must have touched his heart! I did the same thing with the second volume as with the first. Yes, he finished the second volume too, and he began to speak favourably of Christianity. Thank God, he was coming. He finished the third volume, and I observed some change in his life and manners. He would drink less wine, and his behaviour toward his wife and children were [sic] becoming more affectionate than before. The fourth volume was finished, and his heart came down! "Son," he said, "I have been a proud man. From this day, you may be sure, I will be a disciple of Jesus." I took him to a church, and observed in him the convulsion of his whole nature. Everything he heard there moved him. — He would not touch his wine any more. Twelve months more [later], he was baptized. He has studied the Scripture quite thoroughly, and though he never was a bad man, he has been a Christian man ever since. — Jericho fell, and the other cities of Canaan were captured in succession. My cousin, my uncle, my brothers, my mother and my sister, all followed.[17]

In autumn 1881 Kanzo and the others returned to Sapporo, this time to work. Kanzo brought his brother, Tatsusaburo, with him in order to lighten his family's burden, since they were still poor and he was now a salaried man. Tatsusaburo entered Sapporo Agricultural College as his elder brother, Kanzo, had before him.

17. Uchimura, *How I Became a Christian,* pp. 52-53.

4. Founding a New Church

While Kanzo and the others were in Tokyo, Masatake Ohshima, a graduate of SAC, found a house suitable for worship: a two-story structure that had been built as a tenement house. They bought half of this building with a ground area of about thirty-by-thirty-six feet. The ground floor was used entirely as the church, and had a capacity of about fifty.

Upon returning to Sapporo, Kanzo entered his work and started a collective life with his five former classmates in a rented house. In a certain sense, their collective life was a continuation of their college life. Many of them worked mostly outside the town, but when they were in town, they were busy with Christian work. As to the constitution of the church they formed, their creed was the Apostles' Creed, and the church discipline was based on the "Covenant of Believers in Jesus" drawn up by William S. Clark five years earlier at SAC. The church was managed by a committee of five. All common business was conducted by them, but when a matter was raised that the "Covenant" did not touch on, such as the admission and dismissal of members, the entire church membership was called and the matter was put to the vote, with two-thirds of the members needed to carry a motion. Also, since the church did not have a full-time clergyman, Ohshima, Watarase, Itoh, and Uchimura preached in turn. The church attendance sometimes reached sixty. Christian fellows gathered at church on Sundays from early in the morning until the evening service concluded at 10:00 P.M. The church building was also used for classes, and especially as a stopping place.

By this time, union between the Christian churches was being strongly supported by the group. The reasons were as follows: (1) They were schoolmates and had almost the same religious ideas. Therefore, there was no reason for them to worship separately simply because they had been baptized in different churches. For example, Kazutaka Itoh (who had graduated from SAC a year earlier than Kanzo) and others belonged to the Anglican church in Sapporo while Kanzo and others belonged to the Methodist church. (2) It was foolish to have two churches competing with each other in such a small town as Sapporo. (3) They wanted to be free from the restrictions of strict creeds and complicated rituals. (4) They wanted the preaching of the gospel to be done by the Japanese themselves without foreigners' help.

They decided that as soon as they had paid back the money they borrowed from the Methodist mission, those who belonged to the Anglican church would give up their Anglican membership. On the other hand, Kanzo and others who belonged to the Methodist church would submit a report of recession to the Methodist mission station in Hakodate, leaving the Methodist church. Then both parties were to be united and form an independent native church. Under this plan, Anglican members joined the Methodists in their debt-paying efforts. At this time, SAC graduates' monthly net income was about twenty-five yen (U.S. equivalent twenty-five dollars), so their debt-paying effort was not easy. Before long, they received a letter from Davison saying he could not give his consent to the plan of forming an independent church and asking them to pay back by telegram any part of the money his church had forwarded to them to build a house of worship. A little earlier the Sapporo Christians had received a hundred U.S. dollars from William S. Clark in New England for their Christian work. Complying with Davison's requirement, they remitted to him two hundred U.S. dollars by a telegraphic money order, of which Clark's money formed the main portion. Finally, in December 1882, Uchimura and Itoh visited Methodist Mission Headquarters in Tokyo and paid off the difference. Uchimura wrote in his diary what was in his mind when they planned their church's independence:

> They do err who think that our church-independence was intended as an open rebellion against the denomination to which we once belonged. It was an humble attempt to reach the one great aim we had in view; namely, to come to the full consciousness of our own powers and capabilities (God-given), and to remove obstacles in the ways of others seeking God's Truth for the salvation of their souls. He only knows how much he really can do who knows how to rely upon himself. A dependent man is the most helpless being in this universe. — Independence is the conscious realization of one's own capabilities; and I believe this to be the beginning of the realization of many other possibilities in the field of human activity. This is the kindliest and most philosophic way of looking at independence of any kind.[18]

With the independence of the church in Sapporo, Uchimura left the city. Thirteen years later he revisited the Sapporo church and found it in a much more prosperous state than he had left it. Ohshima was still serving

18. Uchimura, *How I Became a Christian*, p. 65.

as pastor, receiving no financial compensation for his church work, earning his livelihood by teaching in the college from which he graduated. The number of church members was about 250. They had two salaried evangelists and a prosperous YMCA. It still kept its independence, not only financially but ecclesiastically and theologically as well. Seeing this, Uchimura was happy. He wrote, "They have a system and principles peculiar to their own, and we believe the Lord wanteth them to retain those peculiarities as sacred. They have a special mission to fulfil, and let no one disturb them in their simplicity and contentment."[19]

5. Broken Marriage and Escape to America

Uchimura said he left his peaceful home church because he felt a vacuum in his heart. "I descried in myself an empty space which neither activity in religious works, nor success in scientific experiments, could fill."[20] A vacuum in his heart: one might say it was caused because he did not know what he wanted to do and felt vaguely alienated.[21]

In April 1883, after a year and nine months as a civil servant in charge of the fisheries, Uchimura resigned his job. In the following month he participated in the Third General Conference of Christians in Tokyo, representing his Sapporo church. In August 1883 Uchimura met a university-educated, Christian girl who was a member of a church — a modern Japanese woman. Uchimura wanted to marry her, but his parents, especially his mother, opposed the marriage. He married her nonetheless, but within six months their marriage had ended in divorce. Historians and biographers of Uchimura have drawn inferences about the reason for their divorce. Uchimura himself wrote in a letter that his wife turned out to be "a wolf in sheep's clothing," and that, with four or five positive proofs of his wife's unfaithful behavior, and after asking his conscience and the Bible for the true solution to the problem, he decided to give her up.[22] We do not know what "the testimonies of four or five" that Uchimura mentioned consisted of. At this time, the Christian churches heavily

19. Uchimura, *How I Became a Christian*, p. 67.
20. Uchimura, *How I Became a Christian*, p. 67.
21. Howes, p. 11.
22. Uchimura to Kingo Miyabe, 27 October 1884, in *Works*, 36:114-15.

blamed Uchimura: firstly, they said, because he did not allow his wife to return to him, even though she regretted her defects; and secondly, because Uchimura divorced her even though she had not committed adultery. They said these two actions were against the teaching of the Bible, and therefore that Uchimura was "a heretic." Masaike thinks these accusations made Uchimura distance himself from the church and indirectly made him stand on Mukyokai-shugi (Non-churchism) in later years.[23]

As a direct result of the divorce and the failure to choose the right occupation, Uchimura went overseas. At the same time, he wanted to see the places where the religion he had devoted himself to was thriving. He planned to go to America first, then London. But as it turned out, he did not go to London. Uchimura sold everything he had and sailed for America, landing in San Francisco, then traveled to Philadelphia.

Uchimura's image of America prior to his trip was, "Where Christianity having had undisputed power and influence for hundreds of years, must, I imagined, be found Peace and Joy in a measure inconceivable to us of heathen extraction, and easily procurable by any sincere seeker after the Truth."[24]

> My idea of the Christian America was lofty, religious, Puritanic. I dreamed of its templed hills, and rocks that rang with hymns and praises. Hebraisms, I thought to be the prevailing speech of the American commonality, and cherub and cherubim, hallelujahs and amens, the common language of its streets.[25]

His image of America was that of "a holy land." In the early 1880s, about twenty years after Japan had been forced to open its door to the outside world, it was natural for a man from an underdeveloped country, as Japan then was, to think of America, then about to become the world's leading power, as "a holy land."

Uchimura arrived at San Francisco in November 1884 and was surprised and disappointed, contrary to his expectation, that the American people used religious words excessively in everyday speech. In everyday conversation, Americans used "by God" and "Jesus Christ!" — words Uchimura would never have pronounced without a sense of extreme awe and rever-

23. Masaike, pp. 92-93.
24. Uchimura, *How I Became a Christian*, p. 76.
25. Uchimura, *How I Became a Christian*, p. 79.

ence. He soon discovered the deep profanity that lay beneath such Hebraisms and took them as open violation of the third commandment of Moses in the Old Testament.

On another occasion, immediately after his arrival at San Francisco, one of his Japanese shipmates was robbed of his purse. Uchimura wrote,

> The report that money was the almighty power in America was corroborated by many of our actual experiences. — Christian civilization was severely tested by a disaster that befell one of our number. He was pick-pocketed of a purse that contained a five-dollar gold piece! Pick-pocketing in Christendom as in Pagandom.[26]

"Indeed, insecurity of things in Christendom is something to which we were wholly unaccustomed. Never have I seen more extensive use of keys than among these Christian people."[27] In one other respect, Christendom appeared to him more like heathendom because of a strong racial prejudice that still existed among the American people.

A few weeks later Uchimura reached Philadelphia. His reason for going there was that William N. Whitney, an American Quaker he had met in Japan, suggested that he visit Mr. and Mrs. Wister Morris. The Morrises introduced Uchimura to a mental hospital in Elwyn, Pennsylvania, where he obtained a job as an attendant for feeble-minded children. Later, he wrote in his autobiography,

> I entered a hospital service with somewhat the same aim as that which drove Martin Luther into his Erfurth convent. I took this step, not because I thought the world needed my service in that line, much less did I seek it as an occupation (poor though I was), but because I thought it to be the only refuge from "the wrath to come" there to put my flesh in subjection.[28]

Uchimura did not elaborate on what he meant by "the wrath to come."

Wister Morris, a successful owner of a railroad company, and his wife, Mary, were Quakers who had an interest in Japanese people. One Saturday a month Japanese students living nearby were invited to their house to

26. Uchimura, *How I Became a Christian*, p. 81.
27. Uchimura, *How I Became a Christian*, p. 83.
28. Uchimura, *How I Became a Christian*, p. 95.

dine with them and listen to a clergyman. The Morrises also gave advice to distressed students, and even financial assistance sometimes. (As a matter of fact, poor Uchimura borrowed his travel expenses from them for his return trip to Japan.) Inazo Ohta (Nitobe), Uchimura's classmate at SAC, visited the Morrises often and is said to have been the first Japanese to become a Quaker. Wister and Mary Morris influenced him greatly while he was studying at Johns Hopkins University. The Morrises as Quakers also had an important effect on Uchimura. One can see it in a letter he wrote upon the death of Mary Morris.

> — And, all these years, I was conscious that she was a partner in my Christian works. She often told me that "thee is almost a Quaker theeself"; and I was always sorry that I was "almost" and not "entirely." Still all my critics recognized in me "a strong Quaker influence," and that "influence" was Mary Morris of Overbrook, Phila — .[29]

6. College Life in New England

After eight months of work at the mental hospital, Uchimura quit his job and moved to New England. One reason he had to quit was his unstable mental condition. He wrote,

> Doubts within me became impossible to be borne for any greater length of time. Relief must be sought somewhere. The good doctor said I needed rest — . Taking advantage of his medical advice, I went to New England where I had some friends from my native land,[30] for I thought something "lucky" might come out by change of locations. My heathen trust in "good lucks" always cropped out when I came to extremities.[31]

Uchimura traveled to Boston, then Gloucester, Massachusetts, a fishing town near Cape Ann. In addition to recovering his health, he wanted to see American fisheries and try to work out his future while he was there. To pay his expenses while in Gloucester, he wrote, in English, a long article

29. Uchimura to Miss Graham, who informed him of Mary Morris's death, 8 October 1924, in *Works*, 39:176.

30. Of Uchimura's SAC classmates, Miyabe was then studying at Harvard University and Ohta (Nitobe) was at Johns Hopkins University.

31. Uchimura, *How I Became a Christian*, p. 109.

entitled "Moral Traits of the Yamato-Damashii [spirit of Japan]." As it
turned out, his article was printed in the bimonthly *Methodist Review* in
January 1886, and Uchimura earned forty dollars from it. In Gloucester,
he decided to devote his life to Christian mission work, and, in September
1885, to begin a course of study at Amherst College, in the central part
of the state. At Amherst he met the president of the college, Julius Hawley
Seelye, who had an important effect upon him. In later years, Uchimura
wrote about Seelye as follows:

> My own teacher in Christian Religion — , Julius H. Seelye, the sixth
> President of Amherst College, was one of the greatest teachers the world
> has had, an essentially humble man, who laid upon the altar of the Lord
> Jesus Christ, his wonderful mass of knowledge, and looked upon Him
> and Him alone for guidance day-by-day. He loved Japan and Japanese,
> respected them, and prayed for them as he prayed for his own country
> and countrymen. Indeed, I could not but bow myself before such a
> man, place the care of my soul in him, and be led by him into light
> and truth. The Lord Jesus Christ shone in his face, beat in his heart;
> and now thirty-nine years after I bade him the last farewell, I feel his
> presence as vividly as when I looked upon his face and heard from his
> lips in the flesh. I promised him that I would report to him in heaven,
> what I would do in Japan. The promise, of course, still remains unful-
> filled; yet it will be fulfilled.[32]

Amherst College, originally founded as a religious institution, had many
professors in religion, and Uchimura seems to have received education of
a high standard there. He attended classes in Christian history, Hebrew,
Greek, and Western history, among others. One thing we should not miss
in Uchimura's experience at Amherst was that he attained to faith in the
atonement of Jesus, with the assistance of Julius Seelye. He wrote in his
diary on 8 March 1886:

> Very important day in my life. Never was the atoning power of Christ
> more clearly revealed to me than it is to-day. In the crucifixion of the
> Son of God lies the solution of all the difficulties that buffeted my mind
> thus far. Christ paying all my debts, can bring me back to the purity

32. Kanzo Uchimura, "Can Americans Teach Japanese in Religion?" *Japan Christian
Intelligencer* 1, no. 9 (5 November 1926), in *Works*, 30:98-105.

and innocence of the first man before the Fall. Now I am God's child, and my duty is to believe Jesus. For His sake, God will give me all I want. He will use me for His glory, and will save me in Heaven at last.[33]

Uchimura graduated from Amherst College in July 1887 with a bachelor of science degree, even though he had been admitted as a non-regular student. Following his graduation, he entered Hartford Theological Seminary (HTS) in Connecticut, but he stayed there for only four and a half months. Uchimura said he left HTS because he was disappointed with the school.

Some of my good friends were sorry of [sic] my quitting theological study without having gone with it so far as to get license. With me, however, license was the thing I was seriously afraid of. And the fear that I had entertained about the bestowal of this new riviledge [sic] upon me grew more as I observed its benefits talked about within the walls of my seminary. "One thousand dollars with parsonage," "Twenty dollars' sermon upon Chicago anarchy," and similar combinations of such words and phrases sounded very discordantly to my ears. That sermons have market-values, as porks [sic] and tomatoes and pumpkins have, is not an Oriental idea at least. We Orientals are [a] very suspicious set of people. — And none we suspect more than who has religion for sale. With us, religion is not usually convertible into cash. Indeed, more religion, less cash.[34]

Uchimura also wrote,

Rather disgusted with works in the recitation rooms. We discussed upon hell and purgatory in New Testament exegesis, and on equally unsubstantial subjects in Apologetics. Spiritless Theology is the driest and most worthless of all studies. To see students laughing and jesting while discussing serious subjects is almost shocking.[35]

The view that Uchimura had no intention of becoming a missionary when he entered HTS is based on this part of his autobiography. He wrote, "I made up my mind to study Theology, but upon one important condi-

33. Uchimura, *How I Became a Christian*, pp. 117-18.
34. Uchimura, *How I Became a Christian*, p. 139.
35. Uchimura, *How I Became a Christian*, p. 135.

tion; and that was that I should never be licensed."[36] However, Tsunao Ohyama thinks this part of his autobiography contains a fiction,[37] for, in a letter to Kingo Miyabe, who was studying at Harvard University at that time, Uchimura wrote, "By the time I go back to Japan I want to be a good intelligent priest."[38] In the other letter sent to Miyabe from Hartford he said, "I wish to become a good intelligent clergyman."[39] Furthermore, in a letter to Julius Seelye from Elwyn, Uchimura wrote,

> I am compelled to write you that my bodily health had been failing to such an extent that I was advised to take a long rest before I resume my study again. I have been losing my sleep all since last June. What I once thought as temporary of fectation [sic] began to take a chronic form. Many weeks I went with sleep of only four or five hours a week. This state of things together with other considerations seem to point me to give up my theological study for a time at least, and to start for Japan at this juncture. I am hoping that by engaging in "practical work," I may be able to regain my health for further study.[40]

For reasons of health, Uchimura could not go back to HTS. Although he had chosen to become a clergyman as his divine vocation, he was therefore unable to complete the course of training required of clergymen in the institutionalized church. Ohyama suggests that this is the fundamental reason for Uchimura's Mukyokai-shugi (Non-churchism).[41] In the course of selecting Amherst College and HTS, Uchimura ascertained that the role of the Christian missionary was his divine vocation.

One thing that should not be missed in Uchimura's experiences in America was his encounter with David C. Bell. In the summer of 1885 Isaac Kerlin, the director of the hospital in Elwyn, took Uchimura to the annual meeting of the Conference of Charities and Correction in Philadelphia. Afterward, the two traveled by carriage to Washington, D.C., to visit

36. Uchimura, *How I Became a Christian,* p. 134.

37. Tsunao Ohyama, "Haatofoodo ni okeru Uchimura Kanzo -Kosho-" (Kanzo Uchimura in Hartford — a historical investigation), *Uchimura Study,* no. 10 (April 1978): 75-84.

38. Uchimura to Miyabe, 27 July 1887, in *Works,* 36:263.

39. Uchimura to Miyabe, 4 January 1888, in *Works,* 36:272.

40. Uchimura to Seelye, 8 February 1888, in *Works,* 36:276.

41. Tsunao Ohyama, "New England no Uchimura Kanzo" (Kanzo Uchimura in New England), *Geppo* (monthly report), no. 4, p. 4, in *Works,* vol. 1.

the White House. In the carriage Uchimura met and talked with a Minneapolis businessman named David C. Bell. The next morning, the two talked further in a hotel lobby in Washington, D.C., and later they accidentally met on the street in Boston. That was all they saw of each other in America. However, their friendship lasted a long time, and Uchimura wrote Bell a total of 184 letters in the following years. After Uchimura's death these letters were made public, offering those interested in Uchimura's movements and thinking information unavailable in other sources.[42]

7. Days as a Teacher

Uchimura returned to Japan by ship in May 1888, after three and a half years in the United States. He had a high ambition in his mind, of serving his people by making his country God's country. Upon his arrival in Tokyo, a job as principal of a school in Niigata Prefecture, a province about 250 miles northwest of Tokyo, was awaiting him. This school, Hokuetsu Gakkan, had been founded only one year earlier and was run neither by the government nor by any Christian mission but by local people — at least that was the story Uchimura was told. It turned out, however, that the salaries of foreign teachers were all paid by an American mission board. Uchimura's letter to David C. Bell in Minnesota shows that six missionaries, including Rev. G. Albrecht from Chicago and Dr. H. M. Scudder from New York, were to help the early stages of the school. Uchimura also taught at the school. He wrote to Bell:

> I explain to them the Book of prophet Jeremiah five times a week. — I do not preach, but give lectures. — We never force, even persuade, the students to bring their Bibles with them; but I see a large number of them — all "heathens" (so-called) except very few — have bought the Scriptures out of their own free choice, and are following me in the Book, taking notes as they go. I believe we are catching those fishes which escape from the nets of common Mission schools. — One important thought which has recently come to my mind is that Japan is Not ready for harvesting. I am afraid Japan is now a spiritual El Dorado

42. Masaike, pp. 110-11.

to churches in all Christendoms [*sic*], where they dream they can reap in "lots of converts" with comparatively very little labor. — True, some ripe wild fruits are ready for harvesting now; but the grains, like those of which you Minn. people are proud, cannot be harvested directly from the prairie. As for myself, I am satisfied with my pioneer life in spiritual Japan. Mine is not to reap, neither to sow, perhaps not even to plow, but to explore, at best to break up the fertile but hard soil. The delightful task "of bringing in the sheaves" I will leave to my brethren of years and years after me. The result of my work I am [anticipating] only through faith at a great distance. You Christians who were brought up in Christian homes and are constantly breathing Xtian atmosphere can hardly imagine what a violent process it is to try to bring "heathen souls" to the conception of the Risen Redeemer.[43]

Uchimura wanted to introduce Japanese religion in general before embarking upon Christian theology. Thus, he invited a Buddhist priest to speak to the students and let a Japanese teach *The Analects of Confucius* at the school as well. Here one can see his principle of Christian mission. However, Uchimura's actions were not acceptable to the very strong-willed Western missionaries and caused serious disagreement between them. Uchimura resigned and went back to Tokyo.

In July 1889 Uchimura married Kazuko Yokohama, a friend from his childhood. In Tokyo he obtained a teaching position in Daiichi Koto Chugakko (the First Higher Middle School; it is the College of General Education at the University of Tokyo today). He taught English, geography, and history. In December 1890, while Uchimura was an instructor at the school, the new Imperial Rescript on Education, with the emperor's signature, was introduced to the school. It reads as follows:

Know ye, Our subjects:
    Our Imperial Ancestors have founded Our Empire on a basis broad and everlasting, and have deeply and firmly implanted virtue; Our subjects ever united in loyalty and filial piety have from generation to generation illustrated the beauty thereof. This is the glory of the fundamental character of Our Empire, and herein also lies the source of Our education. Ye, Our subjects, be filial to your parents, affectionate to your brothers and sisters; as husbands and wives be harmonious, as

43. Uchimura to Bell, 25 November 1888, in *Works*, 36:306-7.

friends true; bear yourselves in modesty and moderation; extend your benevolence to all; pursue learning and cultivate arts, and thereby develop intellectual faculties and perfect moral powers; furthermore, advance public good and promote common interests; always respect the Constitution and observe the laws; should emergency arise, offer yourselves courageously to the State; and thus guard and maintain the prosperity of Our Imperial Throne coeval with heaven and earth. So shall ye not only be Our good and faithful subjects, but render illustrious the best traditions of your forefathers. The Way here set forth is indeed the teaching bequeathed by Our Imperial Ancestors, to be observed alike by Their Descendants and the subjects, infallible for all ages and true in all places. It is Our wish to lay it to heart in all reverence, in common with you, Our subjects, that we may all attain to the same virtue.

October 30, 1890[44]

Analyzed, the rescript's underlying idea is traditionally Japanese, and largely Confucian. Confucian advisers to the emperor had devised it to prevent Japan from becoming over-Westernized. Copies of this rescript were distributed to every school in Japan and hung alongside the emperor's portrait, where all made obeisance to them. In such awe were they held that on occasion teachers and principals risked their lives to rescue them from burning buildings.

On 9 January 1891, at a special ceremony, all students and faculty members gathered at the Daiichi Koto Chugakko and bowed their heads to the rescript. The Christians on campus appear to have been concerned about what meaning would be taken from this act. Would it be interpreted as bowing before a heathen idol? Among Christian faculty members, only Uchimura attended on the day of the formal reception of the rescript; all the others absented themselves. Uchimura might have thought something would happen on that day, for he had written a letter to his friend in Sapporo the day before the reception, telling of his resignation from membership of his Sapporo church.[45] Uchimura was afraid of the effect of the action he intended to take on his home church in Sapporo. As far as we can discover, the principal instructed

44. Theodore de Bary, "The Enlightened Rule of Emperor Meiji," in *Sources of Japanese Tradition* (New York: Columbia University Press, 1958), 2:139-40.
45. Uchimura to Miyabe, 8 January 1891, in *Works*, 36:329-31.

him to bow before the rescript, as in the past Japanese people had bowed before Shinto and Buddhist shrines. Uchimura said he wanted time to think about the meaning of the rescript; he appears to have bowed his head slightly. A letter Uchimura wrote to his American friend Bell on 6 March 1891 offers Uchimura's view about what happened on that day.

> Since I wrote you last, my life has been a very eventful one. On the 9th of Jan., there was in the High Middle School where I taught, a ceremony to acknowledge the Imperial Precept on Education. After the address of the President and reading of the said Precept, the professors and students were asked to go up to the platform one by one, and bow to the Imperial signature affixed to the Precept, in the manner as we used to bow before our ancestral relics as prescribed in Buddhist and Shinto ceremonies. I was not at all prepared to meet such a strange ceremony, for the thing was the new invention of the president of the school. As I was the third in turn to go up and bow, I had scarcely time to think upon the matter. So, hesitating in doubt, I took a safer course for my Christian conscience, and in the august presence of sixty professors (all non-Christian, the two other Xtian prof.'s beside myself having absented themselves) and over one thousand students, I took my stand and did not bow! It was [an] awful moment for me, for I instantly apprehended the result of my conduct. The anti-Christian sentiment which was and still is strong in the school, and which it was a very delicate affair to soothe down by meekness and kindliness on our part, found a just cause (as they suppose) for bringing forth against me accusations of insult against the nation and its Head, and through me against the Christians in general.[46]

John Howes believes that Uchimura's simple hesitation to bow his head became one of the most important events in modern Japanese intellectual history. It is still mentioned in most Japanese textbooks today. It was an introduction of disharmony into a situation that, according to old Confucian ethics, should be harmonious.[47]

Uchimura's conduct on that day became very famous. He became almost a household name as a traitor to the country and had to use an

46. Uchimura to Bell, 6 March 1891, in *Works*, 36:331-32.
47. Howes, p. 17.

assumed name to stay in inns when traveling, because he feared refusal otherwise. Subsequently, Uchimura caught pneumonia and hovered between life and death. Soon after Uchimura recovered, his wife, Kazuko, to whom he had been married for two years, caught the same illness and died. Uchimura attributed her death to the furor caused by his refusal to bow. Later, he described this event by saying that if he had not done what he did, he would have lived the rest of his life differently.

Two years later he wrote a book entitled *Kirisutoshinto no Nagusame* (The consolations of a Christian). Chapter 2 of the book was titled "When Forsaken by His Own Countrymen," referring to the event at Daiichi Koto Chugakko. Incidentally, its first chapter was called "When a Beloved One Passes Away," and referred, of course, to his wife's death; and the third chapter, "When Forsaken by the Christian Church," was about the incident at Hokuetsu Gakkan in Niigata Prefecture. As all these related to Uchimura's own experiences, the book was convincing. Forsaken by Japan and the Japanese he loved, Uchimura's thinking seems to have gone over the Japanese boundary, to the world. In chapter 3 there appears the sentence "I became Mukyokai (No-church)."[48] This is the first time the word *Mukyokai* was used by Uchimura.

Uchimura lost his teaching position at Daiichi Koto Chugakko, left Tokyo, and then went to Osaka and taught in a school. The school, however, having financial problems, was dissolved while Uchimura was still there. One of the board members told Uchimura that they had invited him as an experiment with the thought that maybe he could bring the school together. He next went to Kumamoto to teach English, staying there for three months, before moving on to Kyoto. In the span of five years, Uchimura had changed teaching positions five times. He was nicknamed the "School Breaker." At last, Uchimura said to himself, "I have made up my mind that I shall never enter into educational work, unless I can keep a school with resources which I can use out of my own account."[49]

48. Kanzo Uchimura, *Kirisutoshinto no Nagusame* (The consolations of a Christian), in *Works*, 2:36.

49. Uchimura to Bell, 25 June 1893, in *Works*, 36:379.

8. A Writer in Kyoto

In Kyoto, Uchimura decided to earn a living by writing. In making this decision, he had no expectation of any income and was even prepared for death from hunger. Fortunately, a publisher in Kyoto offered him twenty-five yen a month on the strength of his future prospects. With this, he started to write. One can see what was in his mind in changing his career from teaching to writing from a letter to D. C. Bell in Minnesota.

> It is a sore disappointment to leave educational work after preparing myself for that work many years in America, and being disciplined therein for five years since I returned. The main difficulty with me is that I have convictions upon the matter to which I closely stick, and I fail to find in my country a man of power and influence who can join with me in realizing my ideal. Everybody likes to utilize my experience, but the principle, the strictness, the discipline which I carry into my educational work seem to disagree either with Christian missionaries or with native educationalists. So I am driven to my last resource, to write about my observations abroad, and convictions I came to in my experiences.

In the same letter, he continued:

> I have found out that the utmost I can expect from the most successful book in the line of pure Christian literature in this land is 1,000 copies. The financial standard of the people is so low that a book of 20 cents a copy is a real burden to a large part of them. — The real influence, however, of books in this land is [a] great deal more than might be imagined from the number of copies sold. I believe it is a safe calculation to say that on an average one book is read by at least 10 readers, and the book that sold 1,000 copies, influenced at least 10,000 souls.[50]

In the five years following publication of *Kirisutoshinto no Nagusame* in book form, Uchimura published twelve major works. These are the best known of Uchimura's many books. In December 1893 Uchimura published *Kyuanroku* (Search after peace), which dealt with sins and salvation from sins. Hitoshi Masaike considered it one of the three excellent books

---

50. Uchimura to Bell, 25 June 1893, in *Works,* 36:379-80.

written by Uchimura, and predicted that foreigners in the future would study the Japanese language just to read this book.

Dendo no Seishin (The spirit of evangelism) was published in February 1894. In this book Uchimura describes various types of Christian evangelism: (1) as an occupation, (2) for one's own fame, (3) for the church, (4) for a nation, (5) for God, and (6) for the people. Among these, the first four are described by Uchimura as self-centered evangelism. In the fifth, "for God," evangelism, for the first time, becomes a pure religious work. The danger of evangelism "for God," however, is that the wish to serve God sometimes goes against God. Since one cannot serve God without serving people, the purpose of evangelism is for the people, and to relieve the world from suffering. To become a qualified evangelist, Uchimura said, one must have not only knowledge of the Bible but knowledge of history (including sociology) and science as well. He also pointed out that an evangelist should have knowledge in other areas such as agriculture, biology, and economy. If the evangelist has knowledge only of theology, he may teach divinity students but cannot guide carpenters, plasterers, farmers, merchants, scholars, and politicians. To become an evangelist, one needs thorough study of the Bible, but, in addition, Uchimura said, the ideal evangelist needed to study the Bible in its original languages. Even an excellent translation is no match for the original text. When we study foreign things, dependence on translations is unavoidable, but we should never be content with it.[51]

In May 1894 Uchimura published *Chirigakko* (The study of geography). Three years later the title was changed to *Chijinron* (The earth and man). This book is based on Uchimura's idea that each country has its own mission given by God. Uchimura looked at this question geographically. Six months later he published *Japan and Japanese* (later, the title was changed to *Representative Men of Japan*) in English. This book, according to Uchimura, was written to "introduce Japan to the world and in defence of the Westerners." He picked five representative men in Japanese history: Takamori Saigo, Yozan Uesugi, Sontoku Ninomiya, Toju Nakae, and Saint Nichiren. These were Uchimura's ideal men, and something of these five men's character can be seen in Uchimura's character. For example, according to Hitoshi Masaike, Uchimura's method of Christian mission was

51. Kanzo Uchimura, *Dendo no Seishin* (The spirit of evangelism), in *Works*, 2:307-51. Kanzo Uchimura, "Risoteki Dendoshi" (The ideal evangelist), in *Works*, 1:260-74.

similar to Toju Nakae's educational method.[52] While many Christian churches asked people to come to church, even imploring them to do so, Uchimura limited the number of his pupils, subjecting each of them to a character test before he allowed them to join his meetings.

In May 1895 Uchimura published a book entitled *How I Became a Christian: Out of My Diary,* written in English and published in Tokyo. As he wrote in its introduction, this book describes "how he became a Christian and not why." It is his autobiography, based mainly on the diary he kept while he was in Sapporo and in America. This book is especially written to answer the queries of mission groups in New England. As Uchimura wrote in the preface of the book: "In many a religious gathering to which I was invited during my stay in America to give a talk for fifteen minutes and no more. — I was always at [a] loss how to comply with such a demand, as I could not in any way tell in 'fifteen minutes and no more' the awful change that came over my soul since I was brought in contact with Christianity."[53] At first, Uchimura sought publishers for this book in English-speaking countries, the United States and the United Kingdom, but failing to find publishers there, he published it in the English language in Japan. Later, Henry Revell, the Protestant publisher in Chicago, brought the book out, but the first edition sold only five hundred copies and the book went out of print. Why were so few copies sold? Uchimura describes the reason in a letter to his American friend Bell, written before the book was published.

> The first part of the book has met no objections from missionaries; but the remainder where I speak pretty strongly about some of the dark features of Christendom and [make] some unpleasant observations about missionaries, do not of course please them at all. I know from my own experiences in America that a heathen convert must speak with quite humiliating manner about his own heathendom, and applaud Christendom to call up "pity" from the Christians. That I have never done, however; hence my cold reception in most missionary meetings in your land. Now this book, which is the reflection of my sincere self, is sure to meet the same kind of reception; and though I am not afraid of such, you know it is not very encouraging. Then I fear Mr. Revell will not undertake the publication of such a book, seeing it contains

52. Masaike, p. 246.
53. Uchimura, *How I Became a Christian,* p. 5.

much of heresies, criticisms upon Seminary Life, Vices of Christendom etc. — [54]

His fear came true; the book sold only five hundred copies. But in the United States it was, at any rate, published. In the United Kingdom, he could not find any publisher at all. This book was thus almost ignored by English-speaking people.

On the other hand, in continental Europe it became quite popular. For example, a German edition was published in Stuttgart by Gundert, and went through two printings to a total of eighteen thousand copies. The son of the publisher, Wilhelm Gundert, was so impressed after reading the book that he went to Japan to work with Uchimura.[55] The book was also published in Swedish, Finnish, Danish, and French. It was later translated into Japanese and became a minor classic. It is still read in Japan today. The reason for this success in Japan, John Howes argues, is that it says for the Japanese so many things that they feel and would like to be able to say, but have not been able to put into words.[56]

In 1897 Uchimura published a book entitled *Kosei e no Saidai Ibutsu* (The best memento to posterity). In this work, based on his address at the summer school of a Christian conference in Hakone in 1894, Uchimura said ambition is not a bad thing. "In fact it can be good and can be used for God's ends. It is not a bad thing to earn lots of money and make it available for good philanthropy." He ended his talk by noting that "it is not so much what you do but how you do it. A noble and courageous life is the thing that is most important. This is what every person at the end of his life should like to have had."[57] This book became Uchimura's second most famous work. It is still in print and read in Japan today.

9. The Sino-Japanese War

In autumn of the same year in which Uchimura gave his lecture at the summer school in Hakone, the Japanese government declared war on

54. Uchimura to Bell, 14 December 1893, in *Works*, 36:385.
55. He went to Japan with his wife in 1906 and stayed there until 1935.
56. Howes, p. 19.
57. Kanzo Uchimura, *Kosei e no Saidai Ibutsu* (The best memento to posterity) (1897), in *Works*, 4:292.

China over Korea. Uchimura rose to defend his country before its foreign
critics. He wrote an article entitled "Justification for the Korean War,"
which appeared in the *Japan Weekly Mail*,[58] an English newspaper published in Japan at that time, and in which he explained to Westerners
the rightfulness of Japan's war effort. The article starts by saying there
had been righteous wars in the past. The war Gideon fought against the
Midianites, in which 120,000 were slain by the waters of the Jordan, was
one, and the war in which Gustavus Adolphus invaded Germany to
relieve it from Catholic oppression was another. The American Revolution was also a righteous war, fought on behalf of mankind as the
Americans fought for their independence. However, wars that come out
of "lust" are not righteous wars, because they degrade the divine humanity and are not fought from noble motives but love of gain.[59] Uchimura
believed the Korean war now begun between Japan and China to be such
a righteous war, not only in a legal sense, but in a moral sense as well.
His reason was that Japan as a nation had entered the present conflict
only very reluctantly. At the time of the country's greatest internal prosperity, Japan had wanted to avoid such a war. But China had behaved
in an unneighborly and insolent manner toward Japan for more than
twenty years. While Japan worked to initiate its friendly policy toward
Korea, China worked to prevent it by imposing its own policy on Korea's
regime, endeavoring to keep it as a part of its own system. Uchimura
said in his article that China was a hermit nation, alien to civilization
and the progress of the world. Some 15 million helpless people were kept
ignorant and defenseless merely to satisfy the pride of the world's most
retrogressive nation. Could this be borne by lovers of freedom and ardent
admirers of human rights? The Japanese were not the first to raise their
voice against evil; many other nations had considered the matter before
Japan did, to heal this "open sore of the world." Why, then, had Japan
sent troops to Korea? Uchimura replied that interference itself was not
wrong. Nobody has the right to interfere with his neighbors because of
differences in religion, taste, and trade. But a country has the right to

58. A weekly English newspaper started by William Gunston Howell, a British citizen,
in Yokohama in 1870 as the *Japan Mail*. In 1881 Francis Brinkley, also a British citizen,
became the owner and the chief editor, then changed its name to the *Japan Weekly Mail*.
59. Kanzo Uchimura, "Justification for the Korean War," *Japan Weekly Mail*, 11 August
1894, in *Works*, 3:39.

interfere, and it is her duty to do so, when her neighbors are rapidly going toward destruction. Japan was intervening in Korea because Korea's independence was in jeopardy, because the world's most backward nation was grasping her in her benumbing coils, and because savagery and inhumanity were reigning there when light and civilization were at her very doors. Japan was not disturbing Korea's healthy peace, but acting to save her and free her from glaringly apparent evils.

Seeing China's humiliation was not Japan's aim, but that China would come to consciousness of her own worth and duty, and to friendly cooperation with Japan in the reformation of the East.[60] Thus, Uchimura described this war as a holy war. In April 1895, six months after Uchimura wrote this article, the Sino-Japanese War ended with a Japanese victory. However, when the peace treaty was signed, the Japanese government did not act according to its provisions. Therefore Uchimura became tremendously angry. In a letter to Bell he said,

> The trouble with China is over; or rather, it is said to be over. The war developed all the goodness and boldness in our national temper, and kind Providence gave us a check for the latter aspect of our nature. A "righteous war" has changed into a piratic war somewhat, and a prophet who wrote its "justification" is now in shame.[61]

In the following five months, Uchimura wrote three articles that appeared in *Kokumin no Tomo,* a leading Japanese journal of opinion. They were "Nofu Amos no Kotoba" (Words of the farmer Amos), "Nazeni Daibungaku wa idezaruka" (Why does not Japan produce good literature?), and "Ikanishite Daibungaku o enka" (How can Japan produce good literature?). In "Nofu Amos no Kotoba" Uchimura said he was just referring to the situation in Palestine and what Amos, a prophet, said there around 800 B.C. Therefore, what Amos said had nothing to do with the condition in Japan at that time. However, Uchimura was, in fact, giving a warning to the Japanese in Amos's phrases.[62] "Nazeni Daibungaku wa idezaruka" is a similar warning to the Japanese and their society. In this essay Uchimura said literature is a product of a noble

60. Uchimura, "Justification for the Korean War," pp. 38-48.
61. Uchimura to Bell, 22 May 1895, in *Works,* 36:414.
62. Kanzo Uchimura, "Nofu Amos no Kotoba" (Words of the farmer Amos), *Kokumin no Tomo,* no. 253 (13 June 1895), in *Works,* 3:163-71.

idea. In the first place, good literature is the formation of the universal idea. Japan has not fostered the universal mind, therefore she does not produce a universal literature. "How Japan can produce good literature without having good principle and a decent society to accept it!" Uchimura exclaimed.[63] In "Ikanishite Daibungaku o enka" Uchimura said a poem cannot be greater than the poet. An author's writings are great because the author himself, in the first place, is great. Unless we ourselves become great people, we cannot produce a great work nor a masterpiece. Referring to Thomas Carlyle, a nineteenth-century Scottish writer, Uchimura said, "Without a great cause, he did not write." In short, the answer to "How can Japan produce good literature?" is, according to Uchimura, "above all, by bringing up great men."[64]

10. A Newspaper Editor and the Russo-Japanese War

In January 1897 Uchimura was asked to become an editor of the *Yorozu Choho,* then the largest newspaper in Japan. He held this position for five and a half years, at first being in charge of the English-language column and later a leader writer on current topics. It was during this time that he was in the forefront of social criticism and reform. However, John Howes thinks this period was the low point for Uchimura. Howes thinks the first peak of Uchimura's career was the period previous to his employment on the *Yorozu Choho* that produced his major literary works, and the second high point was the thirty years of production of his own magazine, *Seisho no Kenkyu* (Biblical Studies).[65]

While Uchimura was with the *Yorozu Choho,* the Russo-Japanese War broke out, against which Uchimura, who had supported the Sino-Japanese War ten years earlier, stood up as an antiwar protester. He wrote an article entitled "Senso Haishi Ron" (War-Abolition argument)[66] in

---

63. Kanzo Uchimura, "Nazeni Daibungaku wa idezaruka" (Why does not Japan produce good literature?), *Kokumin no Tomo,* no. 256 (13 July 1895), in *Works,* 3:177-84.

64. Kanzo Uchimura, "Ikanishite Daibungaku o enka" (How can Japan produce good literature?), *Kokumin no Tomo,* nos. 265 and 266 (12 and 19 October 1895), in *Works,* 3:185-201.

65. Howes, p. 23.

66. Kanzo Uchimura, "Senso Haishi Ron" (War-Abolition argument), *Yorozu Choho,* 30 June 1903, in *Works,* 11:296-97.

the *Yorozu Choho* on 30 June 1903, eight months before the start of the Russo-Japanese War, in which he said he was protesting not only against the war with Russia but against any war. In other words, he supported the absolute abolition of war. Uchimura said wars kill people, and killing human beings is a great sin. Therefore, since a nation by waging war is committing great sin, neither the nation nor any individual can benefit from it permanently. Some advocated the resumption of war. He said he had also talked such nonsense at the time of the Sino-Japanese War, but that he had now completely changed and thought advocating the resumption of war was the height of folly. The profit from a war, he argued, could not compensate for the evil of war. The profit of war is the temporary profit of a thief (if there is such a profit), but it is a permanent disadvantage for him and the one who was robbed. The morals of the thief will have degenerated because of this, and as a result, he will have to compensate the sufferer for his loss with several times more goods than he had stolen. If there is the height of folly in this world, it is to guide a nation's development with swords.

His break from the *Yorozu Choho* came when the newspaper decided to support the Japanese government in the war with Russia. Uchimura resigned along with two other columnists, both of whom were socialists. Four months later Japan declared war on Russia. Following his resignation, Uchimura published another antiwar article in his private monthly magazine, *Seisho no Kenkyu,* entitled "Yo ga Hisenronsha to narishi Yurai" (The reasons I became an antiwar protester).[67] He said he was born into a samurai family, so that war was, for him, a hereditary occupation. The stories he had heard and read since he was young were mostly about wars. As a result, he had not been able to understand the evil of war until recently. For the previous twenty-three or twenty-four years, he had been both a Christian and a supporter of war and had, at the time of the Sino-Japanese War, made this public in his article "Justification for the Korean War." Now he wished he had not done so. He had considered Thomas Carlyle's book on Cromwell[68] to be second only to the Bible at that time, and thought justice should be done by the sword in this world. But now his thoughts on war had completely changed. Resisting the words

---

67. Kanzo Uchimura, "Yo ga Hisenronsha to narishi Yurai" (The reasons I became an antiwar protester), *Seisho no Kenkyu,* no. 56 (22 September 1904), in *Works,* 12:423-26.
68. Thomas Carlyle, *Oliver Cromwell's Letters and Speeches.*

of his Quaker friends in America for a long time, he held to his support for war. However, a few years earlier, he had surrendered himself to the views of his Quaker friends. For this reason, some denounced him for inconsistency, but it could not be helped. On the issue of war, he had absolutely changed his principles.

As to what finally made him a pacifist, there were four main reasons.

a. The most influential factor was the Bible, especially the New Testament. By studying the Bible, he finally came to understand that any kind of fighting should be avoided and disliked. Taking the spirit of the entire New Testament into consideration, not picking up words here and there, he came to the conclusion that making war is not right, even if it is an international affair. The gospel of the crucifixion could never justify a war.

b. The second factor that made him an almost extreme pacifist was his lifelong experience. Three or four years before that time some opponents had fiercely attacked him. Following a friend's advice, he bore it standing on a position of nonresistance and, as a result, found great peace in his mind and did not suffer much damage in his work; indeed, as it turned out, he even made many more friends and was helped by them. Then he realized that fighting was very foolish and ugly. He now believed that if he fought hatred with hatred, violence with violence, he might feel some pleasure, but his work would be in vain and he himself might become most miserable. Although all these things were his own concern, he came to understand that all fighting was foolish and ugly. Anybody who experienced the virtue of nonresistance for himself would surely recommend that his nation also put it into practice.

c. The third factor that made him a pacifist was the world history of the previous ten years. The result of the Sino-Japanese War thoroughly convinced him that war was harmful and that no benefit could come from it. The independence of Korea, the purpose of that war, was hindered rather than helped. Morals in Japan, the victorious country, had degenerated. Even though Japan defeated the enemy nation, she could not control those who inflicted damage on her at home, such as the late Mr. Ichibee Furukawa.[69]

69. Owner of the Ashio Copper Mine in Tochigi Prefecture, north of Tokyo. The polluted water from his copper mine became a serious public hazard for the people living along the river downstream. Despite mass protests, the Japanese government did not deal with the matter because the son of the minister of agriculture was Furukawa's son-in-law then.

That was the result of the war (moreover, the result of victory) that he saw in his own country, Japan. He argued that when one saw the result of the Spanish-American War in the United States, one would come to see that it was a serious mistake. By the time of the Spanish-American War, American national policy had taken a new turn. The free country, the United States, was clearly becoming an oppressive country. Though it had once thought only twenty thousand active servicemen were enough for its needs, the United States was planning to become the world's number one armed nation. Along with the changes in American thinking, the corruption and degeneration of their society could hardly be borne. He felt very sad at seeing the degeneration of America at that time, since he kept thinking of America as his second native country, and he held that the direct reason for this degeneration was the Spanish-American War.

d. Fourth was the effect of a newspaper, the *Springfield Republican,*[70] published in Springfield, Massachusetts, to which he had been a subscriber for the previous twenty years. He said he had not read any other newspaper continuously for such a long time, not even Japanese newspapers, and called it, as far as he knew, the purest and fairest of newspapers. It was always calm and reasonable; it was a contributor to cool and unimpassioned thought of a quality rare in the world. And this newspaper maintained a pacifist stance. It was not absolutely antiwar, but it saw all wars with doubtful eyes. It opposed the occupation of the Philippine Islands, contrary to its own countrymen, and continually opposed Joseph Chamberlain, the advocate of British imperialism. "Reading world-famous pacifists' excellent arguments in its newspaper, my hostile, debatable castle was completely destroyed,"[71] Uchimura wrote.

Other forces may have contributed to Uchimura's pacifism, but the above-mentioned four reasons were the primary ones that made him a pacifist.

Westerners commonly believed that antiwar protests were unknown in the history of Japan. In fact, there have indeed been antiwar protesters and arguments in modern Japan. Uchimura was one of these early antiwar campaigners. The Japanese government of the time of the Russo-Japanese War did not oppress pacifists, but allowed them speak out and write freely. Uchimura was visited by the police once or twice during this period, but

---

70. It had no connection with the U.S. Republican Party.
71. Uchimura, "Yo ga Hisenronsha to narishi Yurai," pp. 423-26.

was never spied upon nor subjected to surveillance.[72] Later, the Pacific War (Second World War) was to arouse different attitudes.

11. *Seisho no Kenkyu* (Biblical Studies) and Christian Mission

When Uchimura left the *Yorozu Choho* because of his antiwar convictions, he had no guarantee of a living. In fact, Uchimura said this was one of three times during his life that he was prepared for death from starvation,[73] having only enough money to live for the following three months. He therefore planned to stop issuing his monthly magazine. But fortunately, a royalty of one thousand German marks from the German version of *How I Became a Christian* arrived and allowed him to continue issuing *Seisho no Kenkyu*. Two years after leaving the *Yorozu Choho*, he moved out to the edge of Tokyo to what is now Shinjuku. He lived there for the following twenty-three years, until his death in 1930. During this period, he concentrated on studying the Bible. He also kept publishing *Seisho no Kenkyu*, which had an average monthly circulation of between two thousand and five thousand, as well as giving lectures every Sunday on the study of the Bible. He lived from the subscriptions to his private magazine and charged an attendance fee at his Bible lectures, through both of which he also gained many followers.

In 1914 the First World War broke out. Uchimura was greatly disappointed by America's declaration of war against Germany in 1917, because he thought America could bring peace in Europe as a mediator. At this time, it seems that the vision of the second coming of Christ became more real to Uchimura. In two articles he wrote at this time, "Sekai no Heiwa wa ikanishite kuruka" (How does world peace come?)[74] and "Yo wa hatashite shinposhitsutsu aruka" (Is the world making progress?),[75] he said wars would not be eliminated by human effort, but by God's intervention, which is the second coming of Christ. Uchimura emerged into public life

72. Masaike, pp. 406-7.
73. Kanzo Uchimura, "Dokuritsu Gojunen" (Fifty years of independence), *Seisho no Kenkyu*, no. 335 (10 June 1928), in *Works*, 31:197.
74. Kanzo Uchimura, "Sekai no Heiwa wa ikanishite kuruka" (How does world peace come?), *Seisho no Kenkyu*, no. 134 (10 September 1911), in *Works*, 18:234-40.
75. Kanzo Uchimura, "Yo wa hatashite shinposhitsutsu aruka" (Is the world making progress?), *Seisho no Kenkyu*, no. 134 (10 September 1911), in *Works*, 18:242-47.

once again, giving lectures on the Second Coming both in Tokyo and Osaka for over a year, as well as keeping his magazine going. Unusually for him, he cooperated in this movement with other Christian ministers, such as Juji Nakada and Seimatsu Kimura. This movement lasted for one and a half years. Had Uchimura wanted to continue it, he could have done so, but he did not feel capable of keeping it going. After this time, he preached the second coming of Christ as only one of the truths of the Christian faith.

CHAPTER 3

Why Does Japan Need Christianity?

1. Two *J*s

Uchimura wrote,

> I love two J's and no third; one is Jesus, and the other is Japan. I do not know which I love more, Jesus or Japan. I am hated by my countrymen for Jesus' sake as Yaso,[1] and I am disliked by foreign missionaries for Japan's sake as national and narrow. No matter; I may lose all my friends, but I cannot lose Jesus and Japan. For Jesus' sake, I cannot own any other God than His Father as my God and Father; and for Japan's sake, I cannot accept any faith which comes in the name of foreigners. Come starvation; come death; I cannot disown Jesus and Japan; I am emphatically a Japanese Christian, though I know missionaries in general do not like that name. Jesus and Japan; my faith is not a circle with one center; it is an ellipse with two centers. My heart and mind revolve around the two dear names. And I know that one strengthens the other; Jesus strengthens and purifies my love for Japan; and Japan clarifies and objectivises my love for Jesus. Were it not for the two, I would become a mere dreamer, a fanatic, an amorphous universal man. Jesus makes me a world-man, a friend of humanity; Japan makes me a lover of my country, and through it binds me firmly to the terrestrial globe. I am neither too narrow nor too broad by loving the two at the same time.

1. *Yaso,* the name used for Jesus by the Japanese in the Meiji times, was also used by the Japanese of Christians.

O Jesus,
thou art the Sun of my soul, the saviour dear;
I have given my all to thee!
O Japan,
Land of lands, for thee we give,
Our hearts, our prayers, our service free;
For thee thy sons shall nobly live,
And at thy need shall die for thee.

J. G. Whittier[2]

Uchimura composed his tombstone inscription in English while he was in America. It reads as follows:

I for Japan;
Japan for the World;
The World for Christ;
And All for God.[3]

On 10 February 1903 Uchimura published an article entitled "Shitsubo to Kibo" (Disappointment and hope) in his magazine, *Seisho no Kenkyu*, in which he said,

For us, there are only two lovely names in the heaven and on earth. One is Jesus, and the other is Japan. We are ready to sacrifice our lives for those two lovely names. Jesus is where our future lives are, and Japan is where our lives are. And, since, for those who believe in God, the future and present are the same, Jesus and Japan are identical. That is to say that our faith is for the country, and our patriotism is for Christ. As we cannot truly love the country apart from Christ, we cannot earnestly love Christ if we are separated from the country. The most important reason we believed in Christianity was that we believed it was the only capability which would save the Japan we loved.[4]

2. Kanzo Uchimura, "Two J's," *Japan Christian Intelligencer* 1, no. 7 (9 September 1926), in *Works*, 30:53.

3. Kanzo Uchimura, "To Be Inscribed upon My Tomb," in *Works*, 40:3. Uchimura wrote this in the back cover of his Bible while he was working as an attendant at a hospital for mentally retarded children in Elwyn, Pennsylvania. The epitaph is inscribed on his tombstone in Tama Cemetery in Tokyo.

4. Kanzo Uchimura, "Shitsubo to Kibo — Nihonkoku no Zento" (Disappointment and hope: The future of Japan), *Seisho no Kenkyu*, no. 33 (10 February 1903), in *Works*, 11:49.

Uchimura, who loved Japan so much, was naturally most concerned about Japan's destiny. He quotes the dying words of the English patriot of the Civil War period, John Hampden (1594-1643): "Oh, my God, I pray 'save this my wretched country!' as the cry of all those, of whatever nationality, who believe in Christ. 'For I could wish that I myself were cursed and cut off from Christ for the sake of my brothers, those of my own race, the people of Israel' (Romans 9:3-4) was Apostle Paul's earnest confession. If Japan is saved, I do not care about my own salvation. I do not want to go to heaven just by myself. I want Japan, which I love more than my own life, to be saved."[5]

2. Japanese Society: Corrupted Society

Uchimura saw corruption among politicians, educators, Buddhist priests, Shinto priests, and Christian ministers; fraud, acceptance of bribes, adultery, theft, robbery, murder, venereal disease, treachery, and betrayal were reported in the Japanese newspapers every day. To Uchimura, it seemed that every kind of sin was committed by the Japanese at that time, and nothing was left unaccomplished of the list of sins written in the Bible:

> sexual immorality, impurity and debauchery; idolatry and witchcraft; hatred, discord, jealousy, fits of rage, selfish ambition, dissensions, factions and envy; drunkenness, orgies, and the like. (Gal. 5:19-21)

Politicians had no scruples about abandoning their principles. They were shameless in talking of disgraceful things. The teachers who taught students patriotism and faithfulness to their masters had been thrown into prison on the charge of accepting bribes. While tens of thousands were on the verge of starvation, those who drove them there were enjoying the favors of the imperial court, indulging in luxury and passing their days in indolence. Occasionally someone cried out for righteousness and justice, but his cry was the cry of complaint, not the cry for love of righteousness. The government, in each ministry, had become corrupted. The cabinet, the army, the navy, the Ministry of Home

5. Uchimura, "Shitsubo to Kibo," p. 50.

Affairs, the Ministry of Foreign Affairs — all were corrupted; even the Ministry of Education showed symptoms of corruption. Thus, even primary school teachers had come to think that accepting bribes was a natural thing. Was this not the sign of national ruin? Japan at that time was an extremely insecure society, not in the least trustworthy, nothing but formality, an utterly false society. To the argument that sins were committed not only in Japan, but in the Western countries also, Uchimura said the sins committed by the Japanese were outrageously bad. In Japan truth and unselfishness were merely spoken of; nobody believed in them seriously. Almost everybody in Japan with some experience of the world had a history of tragedy or degeneration. There were neither pure-hearted ladies nor pure-minded gentlemen. Japanese were all flawed articles.

> Ah, sinful nation,
> a people loaded with guilt,
> a brood of evildoers,
> children given to corruption!
> They have forsaken the LORD;
> they have spurned the Holy One of Israel
> and turned their backs on him. . . .
> From the sole of your foot to the top of your head
> there is no soundness —
> only wounds and welts
> and open sores,
> not cleansed or bandaged
> or soothed with oil. (Isa. 1:4, 6)

> Your rulers are rebels,
> companions of thieves;
> they all love bribes
> and chase after gifts. (Isa. 1:23)

This was exactly the state of Japanese society at that time. And the actual conditions were analogous to those of the Kingdom of Israel just before its downfall 2,600 years earlier, described by Amos the prophet:

> They sell the righteous for silver,
> and the needy for a pair of sandals.
> They trample on the heads of the poor

as upon the dust of the ground
and deny justice to the oppressed. (Amos 2:6-7)

Hear this word, you cows of Bashan on Mount Samaria,
you women who oppress the poor and crush the needy. (Amos 4:1)

This condition appeared as a reality in the Japan of 1903. "Israel and Judea
fell because their public officials' atrocities helped their falls. Where are
reasons that Japan would not fall by committing the same sins?"[6] "Japan's
downfall was by no means a figment of the imagination,"[7] Uchimura said.
In these passages Uchimura, in 1903, prophesied the downfall of Japan,
which became a reality in 1945, at the end of the Second World War.

3. Christianity and Civilization

Uchimura said Japan's great difficulty was not the scarcity of wealth, nor
the lack of learning, nor disorder, nor the slackness of agriculture, business,
or industry. Its difficulty was more deep and fundamental. But most
Japanese did not search for the difficulty in its origin; instead they worried
about the scarcity of funds, grieved over the decline of morals, and deplored
the corruption and degeneration of politicians and educators. Japan's
greatest difficulty, the origin of all her problems, was that she had adopted
Christian civilization but not Christianity. Christian civilization is the
civilization springing from Christianity. It does not occur without Christianity, and cannot be understood without learning Christianity. The
Japanese adopted only Christian civilization, but not the origin, cause,
spirit, and life of the civilization, which was Christianity itself. Uchimura
explained the relation between Christianity and Christian civilization by
giving a few examples.

Science

The Japanese habitually say today's science is not the fruit of Christianity;
instead it has advanced despite being constantly opposed by Christianity.

6. Uchimura, "Shitsubo to Kibo," p. 54.
7. Uchimura, "Shitsubo to Kibo," p. 55.

But those who said this, Uchimura claimed, did not know Western history. Many of the great scientists were earnest Christians. In the early days of modern science, those who engaged in scientific pursuit of cosmic phenomena such as Isaac Newton (1642-1727), John Dalton (1766-1844), William Herschel (1738-1822), and Michael Faraday (1791-1867) were all humble servants of Christ. Why had the modern science cultivated in Turkey, Egypt, Morocco, and Spain in the heyday of Islam not developed in its original land, but flourished in the Christian societies of Europe to which it had been moved? Why had science not advanced in the Indian subcontinent, although Indians have keen intelligence? Science is advanced only where the public urges it, welcomes it, and promotes it. In particular, scientific thought, and likewise political thought, do not grow where thought is under oppression. In countries where idols are worshiped science is also not well developed because people's minds are oppressed by the things of this world. Therefore, such minds are not capable of rising above nature and doing thorough research on it. There is a deep correlation between the rise of science and the belief in monotheism.

Education

Anybody who has studied the history of Western education cannot deny the fact that Western education is almost entirely a result of Christianity. Anyone who has read the biography of Johann H. Pestalozzi (1746-1827) cannot deny that he was an earnest Christian, and that his new system of education was thought out of his deep religious ideas. The same is true of Friedrich Froebel (1782-1852) and Johann F. Herbart (1776-1841).[8] If the Christian faith is taken away from Froebel and Herbart, the spirit of their education is eliminated. Where Herbart had written *God*, the Japanese replaced it with the word *Emperor*, because the word *God* was not suited to Japan's national policy. This seemed like true allegiance to the nation, but it was extremely disloyal to Herbart. Such acts should not be

---

8. J. F. Herbart is regarded as one of the founders of theoretical pedagogy, developing Pestalozzi's embryonic ideas into a substantial theory of cognition centering on the process of apperception. Herbart and his followers' contributions were: (1) production of a systematically worked-out educational psychology, (2) bringing the concept of "interest" into a central place in the teaching process, and (3) demonstrating that education could be a carefully considered process of building the minds and characters of the pupils.

carried out by teachers, who are of a sacred profession. The Ministry of Education, instead of condemning such unscholastic acts, enforced the use of the textbook in which the word *Emperor* appears, insisting that it was following the true principles of Herbartian education. However, nature does not forgive such a sin of deception. Japanese education started with falsity, and was already showing the result of falsehood. No teachers took the education of children seriously. They considered education an occupation. Therefore, when they sought a post, they inquired, first of all, about the amount of salary. It was clear that there was neither education as understood by Froebel nor by Herbart in Japan. That is to say, there was no true education in Japan. The educational systems that the Meiji government implemented were all false education. This was because Japan stole the educational systems which among Westerners had been the end result of their ardent prayer and thinking. Then the Japanese selfishly adapted them.[9]

The Constitution

Where did the Meiji Constitution, of which Japan was so proud, come from? Hirobumi Itoh wrote in the constitution's explanatory notes that it was a law system peculiar to Japan. But if that was true, why had representative government not been enacted in Japan until Meiji times? Why did Japan have to learn from the constitutions of Christian countries such as Bavaria and Austria? To say that Japan had a representative governmental system from the beginning, and had not borrowed it from the West, sounded too childish. A Western political scientist who read the Meiji Constitution would laugh at such a view.[10]

Freedom and Civil Rights

Such ideas as freedom and civil rights in civilized countries had not come about without Christianity. Anyone who says that freedom had existed

9. Kanzo Uchimura, "Nihonkoku no Daikonnan" (Japan's great difficulties), *Seisho no Kenkyu,* no. 35 (10 March 1903), in *Works,* 11:152-53.
10. Uchimura, "Nihonkoku no Daikonnan," p. 149.

from the beginning of the world, or that wherever humankind is found there is always freedom, has not investigated the history of freedom thoroughly. There was freedom, as the ancients called it, in early Rome and Greece. But they had not had such freedom as Milton's, Cromwell's, Washington's, and Lincoln's. These men demonstrated a new freedom, a freedom not known to Plato, Socrates, Cato, Seneca, or Cicero. That is to say, this new freedom was introduced to the world for the first time by Jesus Christ of Nazareth. Without him and his disciples, this freedom would never have appeared to this world.

The same could be said about human rights. "Each individual has a right peculiar to himself" does not mean that everyone may do as he pleases. The right is attached to responsibility. As soon as the responsibility is gone, the right attached to it lapses. And a man's responsibility arises from his spiritual relations with God, nature, and men. Without recognizing the existence of God and the actuality of the immortality of the soul, the sense of responsibility crumbles at the root. As a result man becomes a greedy animal possessing intelligence. The sense of responsibility is truly a religious idea. It cannot be explained scientifically. If one wants to maintain the sense of responsibility firmly, he has to rely on the assistance of religion.[11]

Thus, pointing out the deep relationship between Christianity and its civilization, Uchimura makes mention of the condition of Japan in his own time. The Japanese established a constitution, made laws, and founded an educational system, modeling themselves upon Westerners. But they disliked Christianity, which was the spirit, the foundation, and the source of Western civilization, saying they had their indigenous religion and did not need to borrow one from abroad. Or they said, "Eastern ethics, Western science." But nature has its own rules. Even if the Japanese are a great people, they cannot overcome nature. It is not Christianity that punishes Japanese foolishness, heartlessness, and arrogance because it is rejected, but the laws of nature. The Japanese had learned Western science in the last forty years, and claimed that their medicine was by no means inferior to America's or that of European countries. But as the result of forty years of study, what great scientific discovery has been made in Japan? What new philosophical theory has come out? There had not been a single great discovery in the scientific

11. Uchimura, "Nihonkoku no Daikonnan," pp. 149-50.

circles of Japan; but only a few small inventions for industrial use and in pharmacology, and none of them great enough to contribute to the world's science. This was not because Japan lacked a sufficient number of people with innate scientific ability, nor because it wanted research funds. The true reason, Uchimura said, was that "the Japanese scientists or philosophers lacked love for truth."

> There will neither be a great discovery in science made in the interest of profits, nor a great progress in science made for the benefit of one's good name. The truth cannot be searched deeply unless one loves truth itself, parting completely from his greedy mind. A great invention cannot be expected from a scientist who thinks of an invention immediately with the monetary benefits and social honor which will accompany it.[12]

Japanese science is merely the utilization of science. And Japan has almost no science with such a lofty ideal as contributing new knowledge to mankind . by discovering the previously undiscovered truth. Similar things could be said about other fields such as commerce and manufacturing. But one thing is very clear. Christian civilization without Christianity will destroy Japan in the end. China, Turkey, and Morocco were much more fortunate than Japan, because their civilizations suited their religions. Therefore they were not in danger of destruction from their innate self-contradiction. Japan differed from those countries in that her religion was Oriental and her civilization Occidental. Unless Japan corrected this irrationality immediately, she would fall at last by her own self-contradiction. Should Japan in that case give up Western civilization? No, Japan cannot do such a thing. Japan has no choice but to adopt Christianity, the soul of Western civilization, voluntarily and immediately.[13]

4. A Future of Hope

Uchimura, bitterly condemning the corrupted Japanese society, said,

> Indeed, it is darkness. But its darkness is external darkness, not internal. It is the darkness of society, politics, education, the literary world,

12. Uchimura, "Nihonkoku no Daikonnan," pp. 150-51.
13. Uchimura, "Nihonkoku no Daikonnan," p. 155.

government officials, Buddhist priests, riches, but it is not the darkness of God, the land, and the common people.[14]

Decay always means rebirth. The corruption of Japan was the sign of regeneration. The things that ought to die were dying. The morality of loyalty and filial piety that was learned from the Chinese, and the system of education built on it, were crumbling. This meant that the autumn of Oriental Japan had arrived, and its leaves and branches were dying. But beneath the leaves there already sprouted shoots. Therefore, the Japanese should not be disappointed at the darkness of the times: first of all, Japan's hope lies in God's true character. God is a righteous, benevolent God. Therefore, Japan, a creation of God, cannot be a vessel of injustice forever. Anyone who thought that Japan was ruled by feudal clan cliques or by one political party was certain to be disappointed. Japan is the possession of God. God now claims Japan as his. Japan neither belongs to the government nor to the nobility. Japan belongs to God, who created the universe.[15] Since Japan was created by the righteous God to carry out his justice, justice would certainly come into force:

> Stop trusting in man,
> who has but a breath in his nostrils.
> Of what account is he? (Isa. 2:22)

Even though politicians and teachers had gone to the bad, it was too early to give up all hope. The Japanese were living on the land that the righteous God had created. Therefore, the day when their ideal would be realized would certainly come.[16] Another thing to which Uchimura called attention was the disappointment at the lack of trustworthiness and purity in politicians and the nobility. Their circle was called "high society," but in fact it was the most inferior society of mankind from the moral point of view. But if one's expectations were from God, instead of from man, one's mind was always full of hope.

The second ground of hope for Japan lay in its people. Politics in Japan were terribly corrupted, her religion and education were not to be relied

14. Uchimura, "Shitsubo to Kibo," p. 55.
15. Kanzo Uchimura, "Kami no Nihonkoku" (God's Japan), *Seisho no Kenkyu*, no. 148 (10 November 1912), in *Works,* 19:261.
16. Uchimura, "Shitsubo to Kibo," p. 56.

upon. But the Japanese were a remarkable people, and Japan's history proved their excellence. It was an honorable history, and, contrary to many Japanese historians' view, its honor did not lie in the history of the emperor's family line of two thousand years, but in its progressiveness and liberalism. When the Japanese saw good, they could not help but adopt it. For example, they adopted Buddhism, a foreign religion, in spite of many objections to doing so at that time. They were very faithful to the Imperial Household, but they entrusted national administration to capable politicians such as the Hojo family for two hundred years when they thought it was necessary to the trend of the age. Although the Japanese are an island people, they are not satisfied with the islands. Their plans have been always been continental and universal. And if a chance arose, they always attempted to expand to the world. For this reason, when they first came in contact with Western civilization at the reopening of the country in the mid–nineteenth century, they immediately began to absorb and digest it. In a few years, they started running by themselves the machine Westerners took a hundred years to invent. They also showed great interest in the liberal ideas of the West. Although conservative politicians emerged and tried to put down liberal ideas by every possible means, they could not possibly succeed. Freedom and progress were the distinctive character of the Japanese. Sometimes they were forced to put up with oppression, but it usually did not last long. The Japanese race that produced the Crown Prince Shotoku, Saint Kukai, Saint Nichiren, Saint Rennyo, Yasutoki Hojo, Hideyoshi Toyotomi, Gohei Zeniya, and Kazan Watanabe is surely a great race, Uchimura said, with capabilities to achieve great things in the world. "They will not stop until they obtain the world's best and most beautiful things."[17]

The third hope for Japan is found in its land. A country's geographical location (as well as its race) shows that country's mission. Japan, as a gateway to Asia, was charged with a great mission that could unite one half of the world with the other half. Only by going through Japan can China, Korea, India, Persia, and Turkey be saved. Thus, the destiny of more than half of the human race rested on Japan's shoulders. Japan was not created to satisfy the avarice of a few indolent peers and greedy merchants. Japan's reason for existence was to save over 400 million Chinese, over 250 million Indians, and thousands of millions of others

17. Uchimura, "Shitsubo to Kibo," p. 57.

on the Asiatic continent. The hope of Japan inheres in its mission. It was hard to believe that the country charged with such an important mission should stay continuously in such an extremely unsightly state as at that time.[18] Japan's hope was certain as long as Mount Fuji,[19] Mount Chokai,[20] and Mount Asama[21] rise up to the sky, and water flows in the Rivers Tone[22] and Chikuma.[23] The world was demanding a revolution for Japan. Even though the power of the clan faction in the government and of the hypocritical peers was strong, Japan could not reject this demand. Japan would soon accept the great light of the world that is the gospel of Jesus Christ. Japan would, before long, become a Christian country of the yellow race.

And this hope was beginning to be fulfilled now. In spite of very powerful external pressure, the great light was coming to Japan. Despite being ridiculed by its hypocritical society, pure-hearted Japanese were gradually accepting the great light the government officials could not see, in surroundings the peers had never even dreamed of. The Japanese, unlike the Chinese, did not readily admit to their religion when asked by government officials. Nor did they lay the foundation of their spiritual peace by following foreign missionaries. The Japanese neither relied on the government nor turned to foreign missionaries for help, but looked up to Jesus of Nazareth as the Lord. From the most northerly region of Hokkaido to the extreme south of the country, common Japanese people who were honest and loved their country were calling on the name of Jesus, the master of freedom. The government could not obstruct this evangelization even if it enforced laws for this purpose. While teachers who taught students faithfulness to masters and love of country were tied in a row and thrown into prison, the pure-hearted, immaculate, common Japanese were seeking the Lord of cleansing. They were small in number for the present, but Japan's hope was in them. Moreover, they were already be-

---

18. Uchimura, "Shitsubo to Kibo," p. 57.

19. The highest mountain in Japan. It is located west of Tokyo and rises to 3,776 meters above sea level.

20. A mountain located in northern Honshu (main island of Japan), 2,230 meters high.

21. A mountain in central Honshu, northwest of Tokyo, 2,542 meters high.

22. One of the major rivers in Japan. It flows from Lake Kasumigaura to the Pacific Ocean.

23. Upper tributary of River Sinano that runs northward to the Japan Sea in central Honshu.

coming the soul of Japan. The little integrity that had been maintained in Japanese politics was due to them alone. Almost all of Japan's charitable works were following their example. And their future influence would far exceed their influence today. After this social system had collapsed, or after the external form of this nation had temporarily lost its existence, they would rebuild the country on a permanent foundation, and then they would make it an intermediary for the promotion of understanding relations between the West and the East.[24]

24. Uchimura, "Shitsubo to Kibo," pp. 56-59.

CHAPTER 4

Japanese Christianity
and Western Christianity

1. Japanese Christianity

There is no question that Uchimura believed Christianity would save
Japan and the Japanese. The question was, What kind of Christianity?
Uchimura said the kind of Christianity that would save Japan would be
produced by the Japanese in the same way that the Christianity that
saved Germany sprang from Luther and Melanchthon, and the Christianity that saved Britain was Knox's, Milton's, and Bunyan's. This does
not necessarily mean that the kind of Christianity that saves a country
has to be nationalistic, but it has to possess a new vitality strong enough
to sprout out of the old husk. In other words, unless it is a new truth,
it cannot save a new nation. For example, the Christianity (Catholicism)
that saved Italy did not have enough power to save Germany in the
Middle Ages. Likewise the Christianity (Protestantism) that saved America cannot save Japan. Uchimura used this argument to claim that
Christianity imported directly from a foreign land by foreign missionaries
would not be good enough to save Japan and the Japanese. "We might
receive germs of the truth from abroad, but we cannot save both ourselves
and our fellow men with the truth which has not been cultivated at the
bottom of our heart."[1] Japanese Christianity is not a Japanese religion.

1. Kanzo Uchimura, "Nihon o sukuu no Kirisutokyo" (The Christianity which would
save Japan), *Tokyo Dokuritsu Zasshi*, no. 30 (5 May 1899), in *Works* 7:59.

Japanese Christianity is the Christian truth explained from a standpoint peculiar to the Japanese. "It is Christianity received by the Japanese directly from God without any foreign intermediary; no more, no less."[2] Since Christianity is a universal religion, it is molded by each nation's contributions and services. So a Christianity truly received by the Japanese would be a distinctively Japanese Christianity. If a distinctively Japanese Christianity has not appeared yet, this is positive proof that Christianity has not been implanted in Japanese hearts. England produced Episcopalianism, Scotland produced Presbyterianism, and Germany, Lutheranism.[3] As a result there is an English Christianity, a Scottish Christianity, a German Christianity, and an American Christianity; and similarly there could be — indeed, it was already existing — a Japanese Christianity, Uchimura said. Not only England, Scotland, and Germany, but Greece, Italy, France, and America all had contributed great services to this religion. Was it not Japan's turn now?

2. Christianity Grafted onto Bushido

What was the Japanese Christianity Uchimura favored? He said his Christianity was Christianity grafted onto Bushido. In January 1916 Uchimura wrote an article entitled "Bushido and Christianity." It says,

> Bushido is the finest product of Japan. But Bushido by itself cannot save Japan. Christianity grafted upon Bushido will be the finest product of the world. It will save, not only Japan, but the whole world. Now that Christianity is dying in Europe, and America by its materialism cannot revive it, God is calling upon Japan to contribute its best to His service. There was a meaning in the history of Japan. For twenty centuries God has been perfecting Bushido with this very moment in view. Christianity grafted upon Bushido will yet save the world.[4]

Born the son of a samurai, Uchimura's early education was based on Bushido. As he said in his autobiography, he was taught the importance

2. Kanzo Uchimura, "Japanese Christianity," *Seisho no Kenkyu*, no. 245 (10 December 1920), in *Works*, 25:592.

3. Uchimura, "Japanese Christianity," p. 592.

4. Kanzo Uchimura, "Bushido and Christianity," *Seisho no Kenkyu*, no. 186 (10 January 1916), in *Works*, 22:161.

of loyalty to one's feudal lord, fidelity, and respect to one's parents and teachers.[5] Bushido teaches one to be honest, noble, and tolerant; to keep one's promises; not to run into debt; not to run after a fleeing enemy; and not to rejoice at seeing a man driven into a corner. Thus, most of the problems in our lives would be solved by practicing Bushido. But Bushido cannot teach the righteousness of God, the last judgment of God, and the paths toward these. To face these issues, one has to look to Christianity for assistance.[6]

To be a Christian is no less important than being a Japanese *bushi*. John and Paul, the model Jews, turned out to be model Christians. In the same way, those Japanese who give up Bushido, which is the soul of the Japanese, and then make light of it, cannot be good disciples of Christ. In other words, one will not be a true Christian without being a true Japanese.[7] God demands from a Japanese that he accept Christ into the very soul of *bushi*. In this way Uchimura advocated "Christianity grafted onto Bushido."

3. National Religion and Universal Religion

But foreign missionaries in Japan at that time criticized Uchimura's call for "Christianity free from foreign connection," because they thought he was forming a new Christian sect by advocating these claims.[8] They said Christianity is a universal religion, but "Christianity grafted onto Bushido" would make it into a national religion. Uchimura agreed with them but asked whether their Methodism, Presbyterianism, Episcopalianism, Congregationalism, Lutheranism, and hundreds of other Christian "-isms" were all universal religions. Episcopalianism was essentially an English Christianity, Presbyterianism a Scottish Christianity, and Lutheranism a German Christianity. Christians living in the Cumberland Valley of Kentucky had named their Christianity Cumberland Presbyterianism. If they could do that, why

5. Kanzo Uchimura, *How I Became a Christian: Out of My Diary*, in *Works*, 3:10.

6. Kanzo Uchimura, "Bushido to Kirisutokyo" (Bushido and Christianity), *Seisho no Kenkyu*, no. 210 (10 January 1918), in *Works*, 24:8.

7. Kanzo Uchimura, "Kirisutoshinja to Nihonjin" (Christians and the Japanese), *Seisho no Kenkyu*, no. 314 (10 December 1926), in *Works*, 30:59.

8. Kanzo Uchimura, "Japanese Christianity," *Japan Christian Intelligencer* 1, no. 3 (5 May 1926), in *Works*, 29:476-77.

was it wrong for Uchimura to do likewise with the name of his country?[9] A Japanese, by becoming a Christian, does not cease to be a Japanese. On the contrary, he becomes more Japanese by becoming a Christian. When a Japanese truly and independently believes in Christ, he is a Japanese Christian and his Christianity is Japanese Christianity. Paul, a Christian apostle, remained a Jew until the end of his life. Savonarola was an Italian Christian, Luther was a German Christian, and Knox was a Scottish Christian. They were not characterless universal man but distinctively national, therefore distinctively human, and distinctively Christian.[10]

4. Bushido and Christianity

From the late Tokugawa to early Meiji period, many of those who became Christians were samurai or sons and daughters of samurai. During Meiji times Christian leaders such as Jo Niijima (1843-90),[11] Yoichi Honda, Kumaji Kimura, and Tokio Yokoi were all pure samurai. What in Christianity attracted them to the faith? Were there any common features between Bushido and Christianity?

Honesty

Honesy is valued by *bushi*. As a consequence of this, the Japanese had come to hate fraud and craftiness. For example, according to Uchimura, the reason Japanese classical scholars generally disliked Buddhism was that Buddhism lacked honesty in its teachings and Buddhists used indecent means to lead men to their religious awakening. However, there are no such things in Christianity. Christianity was, first of all, honest.[12]

> Rather, we have renounced secret and shameful ways; we do not use deception, nor do we distort the word of God. On the contrary, by

9. Uchimura, "Japanese Christianity," p. 477.

10. Uchimura, "Japanese Christianity," p. 477.

11. Japanese Christian educator who founded Doshisha (later to become Doshisha University) in Kyoto.

12. Kanzo Uchimura, "Bushido to Kirisutokyo" (Bushido and Christianity), *Seisho no Kenkyu*, no. 339 (10 October 1928), in *Works*, 31:293.

setting forth the truth plainly we commend ourselves to every man's conscience in the sight of God. (2 Cor. 4:2)

Thus, fairness is a very important thing in Christianity. The Japanese, reading the words of Paul, the disciple of Christ, strongly sympathize with it. The Bible is, first of all, the book of honesty. It does not have any room to approve of shameful, concealed, or evil events. Moses, Isaiah, Jeremiah, Ezekiel, Daniel, and Amos, later Jesus and, still later, Paul, John, and James — all were men of honesty.[13]

Bravery

When one hears the word *Bushido,* one calls immediately to mind the word *bravery.* Bravery is a very important teaching in Bushido. The Japanese are not afraid to face death for a righteous cause. Compared with this, what does Christianity teach? Many people think Christianity is an unmanly teaching, advocating only love and lacking in courage. However, one who learns the Bible well does not embrace such a notion. If there is womanish Christianity in the world, there is, in contrast to it, manly Christianity. Uchimura did not see Jesus Christ as an effeminate man.

> When it was almost time for the Jewish Passover, Jesus went up to Jerusalem. In the temple courts he found men selling cattle, sheep and doves, and others sitting at tables exchanging money. So he made a whip out of cords, and drove all from the temple area, both sheep and cattle; he scattered the coins of the money changers and overturned their tables. To those who sold doves he said, "Get these out of here! How dare you turn my Father's house into a market!" (John 2:13-16)

This was not a gentle Jesus but a dreadful Jesus. He was unlike Amitabha, and had the so-called anger of the lamb. He was not afraid of men's faces when he cleared the temple courts for a righteous cause. On another occasion, when Jesus was harassed by the people of Nazareth at the start of his missionary work, he neither resisted nor fled from them but calmly left the scene, passing through a hostile crowd, as it is written,

13. Uchimura, "Bushido to Kirisutokyo" (10 October 1928), p. 293.

All the people in the synagogue were furious when they heard this. They got up, drove him [Jesus] out of the town, and took him to the brow of the hill on which the town was built, in order to throw him down the cliff. But he walked right through the crowd and went on his way. (Luke 4:28-30)

This was the bravest act, and this philosophy was also adopted by the Japanese samurai, Uchimura said. Investigating Jesus' actions in the Gospels, he found no case where Jesus was afraid of man and death. The reason people have not become aware of Jesus' courage was that he was a man of love, and there is no case where, confronted by his enemy, he took up a sword and saved himself by defeating that enemy. Jesus' unique courage lay in the fact that he faced his enemy by himself, standing completely alone, entirely unarmed. Only an extraordinarily brave man can do such a thing. And Jesus was not the only man like this. According to the Bible, all men of God were like this. The brave men of faith were all single-handedly brave. They neither confronted their enemy by forming a party, nor depended on the encouragement of their companions' morale. For the sake of truth and righteousness, they exposed themselves individually to the anger of a powerful enemy.

Coming in contact with Christianity, the Japanese, who also have the spirit not to hold their lives dear for the sake of truth and righteousness, have no other alternative but to resonate to the sacrificial spirit of Christianity. That is to say, if the Japanese *bushi* were to disregard their prejudiced views of Christianity, they would be attracted by its nature and become faithful servants of Jesus. Because of this, many Japanese *bushi* became Christians in the early Meiji period; they were attracted by Jesus' *bushi* mind. To them, the education and the article of faith of Christianity were the last matters to be considered. Before anything else, they all adored Jesus' *bushi* character.[14]

Honor

The samurai put great value on honor. Their fear of disgrace was so great that they would choose death rather than be disgraced. Having had the

14. Uchimura, "Bushido to Kirisutokyo" (10 October 1928), pp. 293-94.

samurai's way of life imposed on them, the common Japanese people in general honored their name and valued the life of honor. Similarly, Paul, the greatest disciple of Jesus, said, "I would rather die than have anyone deprive me of this boast" (1 Cor. 9:15). Paul also chose death rather than dishonor. He did not lower his head to others without noble reason. That is to say, he was a Jewish *bushi* in contrast to the Japanese *bushi*. In most cases in everyday life, Japanese Christians who choose to live their lives according to the Bushido that was handed down from their ancestors will not make mistakes even if they do not go to the Bible for consultation. What Bushido teaches does not differ much from what Christianity teaches, with regard to treading the path of righteousness, fulfilling one's duty, being fair, and showing benevolence to the weak.

Independence

Another aspect of Bushido is the spirit of independence. Bushido taught not to go into debt and not to borrow money. And if one has to borrow money, he should pay back what he borrows. "Setting a high value on independence no matter how poor they were" was the foundation of the Japanese *bushi*'s way of life. In Christianity, Paul preferred death to dishonor, dependency, and begging for a cause.[15] Paul said: "The love of money is the root of all kinds of evil" (1 Tim. 6:10). Commercialism, in Paul's view, was the cause of all evil — individual, social, and national. No one was more loyal to his master than Paul. Independent, money-hating, loyal — Paul was a type of old samurai, to be found neither among modern Christians, either of America or Europe, nor even in the samurai's Japan.[16] Thus, the importance of being independent both in Bushido and in Christianity made Uchimura say that if Japanese or foreign missionaries really wanted to make plans for Japanese Christians, they should first of all consider the country's Christianity to be both economically and theologically independent.[17] However, many theologians did not understand

15. Kanzo Uchimura, "Paul a Samurai," *Seisho no Kenkyu,* no. 239 (10 June 1920), in *Works,* 25:362.

16. Uchimura, "Paul a Samurai," p. 362.

17. Kanzo Uchimura, "Dokuritsukirisutokyo ni tsuite" (About independent Christianity), *Yomiuri Shinbun* (Yomiuri Newspaper), 7 June 1925, in *Works,* 29:532-33.

this and did not even try to. Because of his principle Uchimura himself had faced death from starvation. He wrote,

> From the very beginning of my religious life, I made up my mind to be independent. That is to say I believe in Christianity, but will not fall under the command of foreign missionaries. I also made up my mind not to engage in missionary work using money from the foreigners. I have practiced this resolution by and large for fifty years ever since I took up my faith. In fact, there was no other way except to rely on myself because there were very few Japanese who would help in Christian missionary work at that time. I have been on the verge of starvation many times. I have been prepared to die of hunger three times. I always thought that if I could not engage in mission work without asking other men for help, then I would stop it. I am extremely grateful that I have been able to come to this day with my (Christian) faith without starving to death or by having to ask other men for help. Independence is surely the foundation of my faith. By being independent, I found more interests in life, understood the blessing of God, and experienced that God was really living and miraculously rescues those who rely on him. There are some difficulties with being independent, but I found that being independent is far more comfortable than being dependent.[18]

In this way Uchimura encouraged his followers to enjoy the favor of God by making up their minds to pursue independence as he had done.

5. Western Christianity

When Uchimura lived, world power was shifting from Britain to the United States. In Christian circles also, American Christianity and its world mission was coming into its own. For this reason, the influence of American Christianity and its mission had greater power than British Christianity and its mission on Japan. In Uchimura's later years, after the First World War, the signs of decline in Western Christianity started appearing. Uchimura noted this in his writings.

Uchimura said Christianity came out of Asia and is especially suited to

18. Kanzo Uchimura, "Dokuritsu Gojunen" (Fifty years of independence), *Seisho no Kenkyu*, no. 335 (10 June 1928), in *Works*, 31:197.

Asians. All great religions originate in Asia. Religion is a special product of Asia, and Christianity is its greatest product. It is a great mistake to say that Christianity is the religion of the West. The West did not make Christianity. In fact, the opposite is true: Christianity entered the West, then changed it, making today's West. After conquering the West, Christianity went back to Asia again. In ignorance of this clear historical fact, Westerners propagate Christianity as if it were their own religion, and Asians reject it as if it were the Westerners' religion. This is very foolish, in Uchimura's view. It is clear at a glance that Christianity is not an Occidental religion. "Who understands Christianity best amongst the Occidentals?" asked Uchimura. The German Teutons and Russian Slavs, the people closest to Asians in the nature of their hearts. The greater a people's distance from Asia, the poorer their understanding of Christianity. It is obvious to everybody that the Englishmen's understanding of Christianity is much shallower than the Germans'. Those furthest from Asia, the Americans, have the poorest understanding of Christianity. Uchimura was not saying the English and the Americans were insignificant people; they were great in certain things, and Christianity had helped them achieve that greatness. However, the English and the Americans who knew themselves well professed openly that their genius was not in religion. They placed great value on materialism, on politics, and on economics, but not on spiritual, heavenly things and on matters of philosophy and faith. Therefore, their religious movements do not usually start among themselves. For example, Wesley's religious movement, Methodism, had its origin not in England but in Germany, in the Pietist Movement that produced A. H. Francke (1663-1727), P. J. Spener (1635-1705), and others. The deep faith that Germans have cannot be found among the English or the Americans. Among Westerners, the rich spiritual nature of Asians is found only in Germans, and probably Russians. Reading the works of German philosophers and theologians, coming into contact with coolheaded thinkers such as Kant, Jacobi, and Hegel, one immediately feels that they have a deep spiritual nature. German philosophers are generally idealistic, because it is in their nature to be so. They place emphasis on the inner life, on the mind and inner self. They see man mainly as an existence of will, relying less on outward nature and more on inner strength. Therefore their faith naturally comes from within and is spiritual.

On the other hand, the religion of Englishmen and Americans relies more on outwardness and less on inner strength. The English and Americans value numbers; statistics is their means of proving the truth. To them, the religion with the most followers is the best religion. Their faith is expressed immediately in a movement. They despise a faith that can be enjoyed by just believing, and call it mysticism. Even in matters of faith, they think great things cannot be done without the help of money. They place the emphasis on external influences and make light of willpower. They emphasize the effect of external influences and think that without the improvement of environmental conditions human minds cannot be reformed. Americans know all too well that religion is not their genius. Christianity is a spiritual religion. Jesus said, "What good will it be for a man if he gains the whole world, yet forfeits his soul?" (Matt. 16:26). Christ teaches that if one gains enormous wealth, cars, airplanes, radios, great naval forces that dominate the whole Pacific, a sea of gold that one can float one's body in, yet forfeits one's soul, what good will it be?[19]

America and American Christianity

Uchimura said Christianity taught by foreigners, especially Americans, could not possibly save Japan and its people. Why not? One reason was that American Christianity was materialistic and worldly.

Americans were great people, Uchimura said. They planned and acted on a big scale and accomplished what they set out to achieve. He had learned many things from the Americans, and owed much to them. However, the Americans, like all other peoples on earth, were not a perfect people. They had many faults, and it was important for both Japanese and Americans to recognize this. Americans are good at building cities and railroads; have a wonderful genius for improving breeds of horses, cattle, sheep, and swine; are great inventors — originating or perfecting telegraphs, telephones, automobiles, and even poisonous gases — and are adept at enjoying life to the full. They are also good at democracy,[20] and their ideal government is a government without a king. But, although they dislike kings and emperors, they live like kings and emperors. In other words, they love freedom, but at the same time they want to make others exactly the same as they are.

19. Kanzo Uchimura, "Nihonkoku to Kirisutokyo" (Japan and Christianity), *Seisho no Kenkyu*, no. 301 (10 August 1925), in *Works*, 29:271-78.

20. Kanzo Uchimura, "Can Americans Teach Japanese in Religion?" *Japan Christian Intelligencer* 1, no. 9 (5 November 1926), in *Works*, 30:98-105.

Americans are great in the matters of this world, but do not excel in matters of religion or high philosophy.[21] This can be proved by the fact that America, despite its great wealth, has not produced a single great philosopher, the equivalent of a Kant, a Spinoza, or a Leibniz. The greatest philosopher America has produced is William James (1842-1910), the leader of Pragmatism; but he was a psychologist, said Uchimura, rather than a philosopher. It is hard to imagine that America could produce a great, dynamic philosopher who searches for the truth of the universe deeply and spiritually. Furthermore, America has not produced a great artist or a great musician. In this respect, powerful America is no match for small Denmark or Sweden. America has many great paintings now, but these are the works of foreign artists that Americans purchased with large sums of money. Americans produced wealthy men such as J. J. Astor, J. Gould, J. P. Morgan, and J. D. Rockefeller, but not a Vereshchagin, a Millet, or a Munkácsy. The whole world, and especially the religious East, feels that they are not to be taught by Americans in religious matters. For Americans, religion is movement; they do not understand the meaning of pure faith such as "In returning and rest you shall be saved; in quietness and in trust shall be your strength" (Isa. 30:15, NRSV). Also, the faith of John and Paul, the Christian disciples, cannot be seen among Americans. On the point of attending to statistical results more than to faith itself, American faith is all the same. There is no difference between the Catholics and the Protestants. Americans possess a form of faith, but deny its real power.[22]

Christendom and Its Missionaries

We read of David Livingstone (1813-1873) winning the hearts of the Kaffirs and the Matabeles. Gordon, Schwartz, and men and women of their character won the genuine love and respect of the people among whom they lived. William Penn's "holy experiment" with the American Indians was decidedly successful, and there was no need for him to vin-

---

21. Kanzo Uchimura, "Americans as Teachers," *Seisho no Kenkyu*, no. 183 (10 October 1915), in *Works*, 21:449.

22. Kanzo Uchimura, "Nihon no Tenshoku" (The mission of Japan), *Seisho no Kenkyu*, no. 292 (10 November 1924), in *Works*, 28:406.

dicate his right upon the American soil with fire and sword. However, Uchimura said, missionaries may have converted some people to Christianity in foreign lands, but there is no single case of a whole country being saved by them. On the contrary, they destroyed countries in many cases.[23] Beginning with Montezuma's Mexican and the Peruvian Incan empires, Christendom's course has always been absorption, destruction, and, in some cases, even annihilation. It has killed India — politically, at least. It has killed Burma and Annam. It has killed Hawaii after keeping it alive for some forty years. It will yet kill Abyssinia, Egypt, and Morocco. What securities are there against missionaries killing China and Korea, and even Japan as well, when opportunities are offered to them? The killing is not necessarily done with guns and bayonets, but by other means. Western Christendom kills non-Christian countries by introducing rum and whiskey, and tobacco; by its many foul diseases; and by its atheism, nihilism, and other destructive isms. Christendom is bound by its moral code to help heathendom, as the elder brother is bound to help the younger. It does not deserve its own name until it can do this.

Sectarianism

One of the reasons Uchimura took precautions against Western Christianity was that it was sectarian. He became aware of "the evil of denominationalism" when he encountered Christianity for the first time in Sapporo as a student. For Uchimura, therefore, the Christianity that takes root in Japanese soil must be Christianity without sectarianism. Thus, it could also be said that the reason Uchimura disliked European and American missionaries was that he hated their sectarianism. He wrote,

> Who are more sectarian than the people of the West, of America and Europe, especially they of the Anglo-Saxon descent, and those who come under their influence? Sectarianism seems to be in the very make [sic] of their being. Every one of them seems to believe that he or she is right in politics and in religion. Their government is carried on by parties; it is called party-government; we may just as well call it sectarian govern-

---

23. Kanzo Uchimura, "Christendom versus Heathendom," *Yorozu Choho,* 17 March 1897, in *Works,* 4:59-60.

ment. Every Democrat is absolutely sure that he is right in his views on government; and he considers it his patriotic duty to convert all Republicans to his, i.e. Democratic party. And vice versa. And as in politics, so in religion. Every Englishman or American has his church or no-church. He is absolutely sure that his views in religion are right as in politics; and he considers it his bounden duty to convert all others, — the whole world, if he can, — to his views on God, Life and Eternity. So, though they call themselves Christians, there are practically as many kinds of Christianity as their number, every one of them forming a sect by himself, and trying to make all others believe just exactly as he does. Roughly, they are divided into churches, which are practically religious parties; only parties religious are more numerous than parties political.[24]

It was said that in the city of London in Uchimura's time, there were some six hundred different Christian churches. Moreover, one main church had dozens of divisions. For example, Methodism was represented by a great number of Methodist churches: the Protestant Methodist Church, the United Methodist Church, the Primitive Methodist Church, the Calvinistic Methodist Church, the Methodist Episcopal Church–North, the Methodist Episcopal Church–South, the Canadian Methodist Church, etc. The same could be said of Presbyterian, Baptist, and more or less of Anglican and Lutheran churches. In addition, every one of them claimed to be in possession of the absolute truth; every one had one or more missionary societies to bring not only poor benighted heathen, but also other Christians differently persuaded, to its own fold. The heathen was assured of full salvation in different ways by different missionaries. The Anglican missionary was not at all satisfied with the Methodist convert; the poor convert must be re-converted to the Holy Catholic Church, as the Anglican missionary called his own church, to be assured of heaven and eternal bliss. All missionaries agreed on one thing, Uchimura claimed: they could not permit Christianity without churches. But when it came to the choice of churches, they each claimed their respective churches to be the best and only reliable one. This was the state of Christianity in the West.

Someone had called Christianity the religion of humanity, Uchimura said. However, sectarianism is the opposite of humanity. It possesses an arrogance approaching that of the evil one, who presumes perfection in himself alone.

24. Kanzo Uchimura, "Again about Sectarianism," *Japan Christian Intelligencer* 2, no. 9 (10 November 1927), in *Works*, 30:477.

Sectarianism is opposed to the very spirit of Christianity because Christ is not divided. Even if division is unavoidable under the present circumstances, the divided members should love and respect one another.[25]

Mission School and Mission School–Trained Christians

Uchimura said that if he had twenty children, he would not send even one to mission school.[26] What made Uchimura say this? Although missionaries wished to produce believers, what they did produce, he said, were terrible hypocrites, people who acted like and thought they were believers, and thus had the least chance of repentance. According to Uchimura, these believers sing well, pray well, encourage others, and even cry very well. However, they do not even know the elementary mind of Jesus Christ. There is nothing in man's spiritual life more dangerous than "having a form of godliness but denying its power" (2 Tim. 3:5). In other words, the so-called believer that the mission school produces is one who plays the faith on the social scene, and is an actor of the faith, having a form of godliness but denying its power, learning the faith as an art but not attaining the faith itself. Uchimura would rather his children be pure unbelievers than such Christians. For an unbeliever, there is a hope of being converted to a believer, but to turn an actor into a true believer is almost impossible. Actors know everything about faith; therefore they know nothing about it. There is nothing more dangerous than leaving children in the care of such missionaries who learn Christianity by habit, and then introduce it to heathens. That is putting children in danger of destroying their souls.[27]

6. The Future of Christianity in Japan

According to Uchimura, the true crisis of faith in Japan would come after Japan had become a Christian country. It would come when bishops were

25. Uchimura, "Again about Sectarianism," pp. 477-78.
26. Kanzo Uchimura, "Seishuzakkan" (Miscellaneous thoughts on a fine autumn day), *Seisho no Kenkyu*, no. 230 (10 September 1919), in *Works*, 25:134.
27. Uchimura, "Seishuzakkan," pp. 134-35.

granted titles of nobility and ministers were honored with court rank. If matters continued progressing as they were at Uchimura's time, such a time would surely come.[28] And it was to be most feared, and to be cursed. After Christianity achieved success in Japan, the government would adopt it. Gentlemen of high social rank would, with their families, seek to be christened and strive to be foremost. Bishops, ministers, and missionaries would be appointed by the government and would live in ease and comfort on government salaries. The Buddhist temples would be turned into Christian churches, and Buddhist priests would keep their hair and wear a frock coat instead of Buddhist clerical robes. They would read the Bible just as they now read the Buddhist scriptures. As a result of all this, hypocrisy would be even more outrageous than it was in the Christian churches of Uchimura's day. During such times those who openly opposed Christianity would be severely persecuted by both the government and the people. The degeneration of faith would become progressively greater. Therefore, one who truly loved the truth and valued humanity would become an atheist, abandoning Christianity, and would then vigorously attack the government and churches. That is to say, "if Japan in the future turned into a so-called Christian country, as today's Italy, Austria, Germany, Russia, England, and the United States are, the people would dare to do anti-Christian acts while hoisting up the flag of the cross, as those Christian countries do today."[29]

With this in mind, Uchimura said he thanked God that he was born in non-Christian Japan instead of the coming Christian Japan. Meeting with government hatred and public opposition would be much better than being persecuted by them in the name of Christ. He could maintain his faith as a follower of Christ in the present time, but a hundred years later he would have been obliged to forsake it and stand against Christian hypocrisy in order to follow a clear conscience, just as Robert G. Ingersoll of America and Charles Bradlaugh of England had done. Taking this into consideration, "matters like the hardship of life and inhospitability of society were not even worth considering."[30]

Looking at Japan closely at that time, Uchimura found that true Chris-

28. Kanzo Uchimura, "Nihon ni okeru Kirisutokyo no Shorai" (The future of Christianity in Japan), *Seisho no Kenkyu*, no. 135 (10 October 1911), in *Works*, 18:286.

29. Uchimura, "Nihon ni okeru Kirisutokyo no Shorai," p. 286.

30. Uchimura, "Nihon ni okeru Kirisutokyo no Shorai," p. 286.

tians were growing up there. He claimed the Japanese were religious people by nature and possessed the greatest depth of religious faith in the world. The proof of this could be seen in the flourishing Shinto shrines and Buddhist temples and in the strong sense of respect the people had for deities and Buddha. However, since these old religions had lost their true capability to guide and influence the Japanese people, the Japanese were now looking for something else to fulfill their religious needs. It had been hard to accept Christianity before now because of government policy, especially the policy of the Ministry of Education. But nobody, even powerful politicians, could prevent the desire of people's souls. The Japanese had been accepting the gospel of Christ reluctantly, but when they came to believe in Christianity from the bottom of their hearts, Japan would become the best Christian country in the world, the world leader, Uchimura claimed.

It had been said that Christianity in Japan depended entirely on foreigners, and therefore, when foreign aid was cut off, Christianity in Japan would collapse. This was a possibility for some Christian sects, Uchimura said. However, there surely was a Christianity the Japanese believed in, a Japanese Christianity, a Christianity that had no dependence on foreigners' support.[31] (Interestingly, a foreign missionary who had been stationed in Japan reported at the World Missionary Conference in Edinburgh in 1910 that there were Japanese ministers who were independent in thought and action.)[32] The existence of such a Japanese Christianity did not depend on the presence of foreign aid at all, but existed as Japanese ardor existed. As Buddhism, once a foreign religion, had become a Japanese religion, Christianity had already undoubtedly become a Japanese religion, Uchimura said.[33] It was to Japan's honor and proof of the power of Christianity that there was such an independent Japanese Christianity, existing without foreigners' assistance, and actually hated by the foreigners. However, Christianity was also hated by some fellow countrymen, who saw it as a foreign religion, ruining the national policy and running contrary to the morals peculiar to Japan. The faith, however, had a firm foothold in Japan. The

31. Kanzo Uchimura, "Kirisutokyosenden to Nihonbunka" (Christian mission and the Japanese culture), *Taiyo* 26, no. 11 (1 October 1920), in *Works*, 25:555-56.

32. William Imbrie, "The Missionary Message in Relation to Non-Christian Religions," *Proceedings of the World Missionary Conference in Edinburgh* (Edinburgh, Scotland, 1910), p. 84.

33. Uchimura, "Kirisutokyosenden to Nihonbunka," p. 556.

Holy Spirit had already left America and Europe and seemed to be searching for new places. Because of this, Christianity in Japan had increased in importance in the world's Christian circles. Uchimura interpreted this as a sign of God's will and that God was preserving his teaching through the Japanese people, using them as missionaries, as he had Uchimura himself. This was the very task that was the most important mission of Japan to the world. Uchimura even said Japan hereafter must go to America to teach the people.[34] The Americans would grow angry with the Japanese, saying, "You were born in sin; how dare you lecture to us!" just as the Pharisees told the blind man in the New Testament (see John 9:34). For Japan, the period of being taught by foreigners in this matter had passed, Uchimura said. Japan, burdened with the responsibility, must become increasingly humble. In bearing the responsibility of serving foreign countries with the faith granted directly from God, Japan must not receive financial help from abroad, Uchimura repeatedly stressed.[35]

34. Kanzo Uchimura, "Nihon to Kirisutokyo" (Japan and Christianity), *Dokuritsu-shinpo,* no. 177 (15 October 1927), in *Works,* 30:561.
35. Uchimura, "Nihon to Kirisutokyo," p. 561.

CHAPTER 5

Uchimura's View on Institutional Churches

1. Uchimura and the Church

In June 1878 Uchimura and six Sapporo Agricultural College (SAC) classmates received baptism from Rev. Mirriam Colbert Harris, a Methodist Episcopal missionary from the United States, and started their own church in their dormitory room. After graduating from SAC in 1881, Uchimura and other SAC graduates founded the Sapporo Independent Church.

In January 1891, at Daiichi Koto Chugakko, a government school in Tokyo where Uchimura was employed as a teacher, Uchimura refused as a Christian to bow his head at the reading of the Imperial Rescript on Education signed by the emperor. Faculty members[1] and students[2] attending the ceremony immediately stood up against Uchimura's action, and it subsequently led to a fierce national controversy over the loyalty of Christians and created serious disturbances at the school. The principal of the school, Koji Kinoshita, wrote Uchimura a letter suggesting that he make a bow to the rescript with the emperor's signature to calm down the students at the school. (Making a bow to the rescript was not worshiping the emperor as God, Kinoshita said, but merely paying one's respect.) After Uchimura received the letter, he consulted on the matter with four Chris-

---

1. About sixty faculty members were in attendance.
2. About one thousand students were in attendance.

tian friends — two Christian teachers at the school, Uchimura's colleagues, who absented themselves from the reading of the rescript; and two Protestant ministers — and eventually decided to accept the principal's suggestion. By then, however, Uchimura had fallen seriously ill. Therefore, Shunkichi Kimura, one of his Christian colleagues at the school, bowed to the rescript on his behalf on 29 January 1891. However, this conduct brought criticism from the Nihon Kirisuto Kokai (the Church of Christ in Japan), which said Uchimura had acted in a cowardly fashion, allowing Kimura to bow to the rescript for him. Despite this, Uchimura was forced to resign from his position by the government and was called a traitor to the nation.

One day before the reading of the Imperial Rescript on Education, on 8 January 1891, Uchimura had written a letter to the Sapporo Independent Church, withdrawing his membership. He seemed to have had a presentiment that something would happen the following day and did not want to bring trouble, by his action, upon the congregation.[3] So, after his refusal to bow, with no safe place to live in Japan, Uchimura returned to Sapporo, a hometown in his mind, expecting comforting words from his old friends from SAC. But when he got there in May 1891, none of them was friendly to him. One even said, "Uchimura has done a stupid thing."[4] Uchimura went back to Tokyo disappointed and miserable, called a traitor to the nation and forsaken by his old friends and Christian churches.

Between 1891 and 1900, Uchimura had no church to belong to. During these nine years, Tokio Yokoi, a Congregational minister in Tokyo, encouraged Uchimura to join his church, and Uchimura, given the cold shoulder at Sapporo Independent Church, seems to have tried to join the Congregational church in or around 1891. However, there is no proof that Uchimura actually joined the Congregational church in

3. In feudal Japan, individual right was not acknowledged. Therefore, for one guilty of an antisocial action, persecution applied not only to himself but extended to his relatives, friends, and the organizations he associated with. In such a social environment, one who committed an antisocial action cut off all relations beforehand to avoid persecution reaching his relatives. Even Meiji Japan, more modernized than during the feudal Tokugawa period, exhibited such a tendency. For this reason, Uchimura wrote a letter to the Sapporo Independent Church beforehand, to prevent persecution reaching them.

4. Hitoshi Masaike, *Uchimura Kanzo Den* (The life of Kanzo Uchimura) (Tokyo: Kyobunkan, 1977), p. 192.

Tokyo.[5] Hitoshi Masaike believes Yokoi's attempt was unsuccessful because of opposition from the leading members of the church.[6] Yokoi,
however, showed Uchimura sympathy by giving him the opportunity to
lecture on the Bible at his church, thus allowing Uchimura to gain some
income.

After these years, Uchimura gradually developed the Mukyokai-shugi.
The word *Mukyokai* (Non-church) appeared, for the first time, in
Uchimura's book *Kirisutoshinto no Nagusame* (The consolations of a
Christian), published in February 1893. The term *Mukyokai-shugi* (Non-
churchism) was first used by Uchimura in his article "Mukyokai-shugi no
Zenshin" (The advancement of the Mukyokai-shugi) in *Seisho no Kenkyu*
(Biblical Studies) in March 1907.

2. Definition of the Church

Uchimura said the church was neither the church building, the institutional system, nor an organized body that wielded power. The church is
"where Christ dwells in the human soul, and where two or more such
people gather together in Christ's name."[7] As Jesus himself said, "Where
two or three come together in my name, there am I with them" (Matt.
18:20). The church is really very simple. Its center is Christ, and the people
gathered around him are those who wish to do things in his way. Thus,
wherever Christ is there is a church. "Two or three" is by no means a large
number — two is good enough.

Originally, the word *church* came from the Greek word *ekklesia*. It is
the name given to the people who are chosen and called by God. The
origin of the word *church* in English and *Kirche* in German is different
from *ekklesia*. Both originally came from the Greek word *kyriakon*, which
means "the house of God." It was a purely religious word that had the

---

5. Masaike, p. 193.

6. Masaike suspected that the Congregational Mission Board objected to Uchimura's
admission to the Congregational church because Uchimura was the one who caused trouble
with the Congregational missionaries from the United States at Hokuetsu Gakkan, where
he was principal in 1888.

7. Kanzo Uchimura, "Honto no Kyokai" (The true church), *Reiko*, no. 2 (10 November
1921), in *Works*, 26:534-35. Kanzo Uchimura, "Kyokai to Fukuin" (The church and the
gospel), *Dokuritsushinpo*, no. 200 (15 September 1929), in *Works*, 32:200-201.

meaning of "temple" or "chapel," unlike *ekklesia,* which originally meant "the meeting of ordinary people."

Christ rarely used a word that has been translated "church." The four Gospels in the New Testament, which tell of the speech and conduct of Christ, do not record the word except in Matthew, where it is mentioned only twice. Mark and Luke do not mention this word at all. John, the disciple of Christ who was said to be the founder of the institutional church, and author of a Gospel and three Epistles, did not touch on the matter of the church at all, not even once. From this, it is clear how difficult it is to seek the origin of the church in the mind of Christ. It is also clear that the meaning of the word changed over many years until it finally came to mean the "institutional church."

One passage in which Christ mentioned the church was this:

> If your brother sins against you, go and show him his fault, just between the two of you. If he listens to you, you have won your brother over. But if he will not listen, take one or two others along, so that "every matter may be established by the testimony of two or three witnesses." If he refuses to listen to them, tell it to the church; and if he refuses to listen even to the church, treat him as you would a pagan or a tax collector. (Matt. 18:15-17)

As it is placed in the context of this sentence, it is obvious that *ekklesia* should not always be translated the "church." If a person is not willing to be told his faults by a brother, he should be taken to two or three others. If he still refuses to listen, his fault should be told to an assembly. This means that the opinion of a large number of people should be taken on the matter, but it does not mean putting the person on trial in church. Jesus therefore used the word *ekklesia* in the ordinary sense of "assembly."

Another passage is Matthew 16:18: "And I tell you that you are Peter, and on this rock I will build my church." Christ certainly did not use Greek in his sermon. Therefore, it is clear that these words, which are recorded in Greek in the New Testament, were a translation by the apostles of Christ. What word did Christ speak that was translated *ekklesia?* It is pointless to investigate this today. Assuming his disciples' translation was correct, it is clear, from reading the verse, that Christ was not referring to today's so-called church. Jesus said he would build his unique congregation on the basis of Peter's confession to him, "You are the Christ. . . ." These are the only two instances in which Christ mentioned the church. If the Bible had not mentioned the church any more, it would have been good for posterity, Uchimura said.[8]

Contrary to their Master's teachings, the apostles put emphasis on the church and, as a consequence, today's church came into existence. The person chiefly responsible for this unsatisfactory outcome was the apostle Paul. He laid the foundation for today's church and, through him, both the institutional church and theology came into being. For Paul, *ekklesia*, in a literal sense, meant a group formed from people who were called by God. He himself was a disciple who was called, and all the believers were those who were called. To him, all Christians were *kletos*, that is, "those who were called," and *ekklesia* was a party that was formed by them. The church was naturally formed by those who were chosen and called by God. Thus, its proposal, establishment, and perfection were all dependent on God. "And the Lord added to their number daily those who were being saved" (Acts 2:47). This means that the church is not a party formed by those who cleansed themselves and then served the Lord, but by those who were chosen and saved by God. They were drawn to each other and cooperated with each other, and then formed a party. Paul therefore told an elder in Ephesus: "Be shepherds of the church of God, which he bought with his own blood" (Acts 20:28). Therefore, the church was, in every way, the church of God. It should neither be established, controlled, nor ruled over by men. Further, Paul called the church "[Christ's] body, the fullness of him who fills everything in every way" (Eph. 1:22-23). This means that the church is where people are filled with the spirit of Christ. In other words, there must be the church of Christ, but it is invisible, just as the kingdom of God is invisible. Its head, Christ, is in heaven, and is seated on the right side of the Father. His body was once dead, but was resurrected. Thus, studying Paul's view on the church in depth, it is clear that the church he mentioned was far removed from the church on earth. However, Paul's view on the church was easily misunderstood. A few years after his death, or even while he was still alive, the *ekklesia* he established became an entirely worldly church. Uchimura holds that, by changing from the spiritual *ekklesia* to the visible church, it became entirely vulgar.

---

8. Kanzo Uchimura, "Ekurejia — Kyokai to yakuserareshi Gengo" (Ekklesia — the original word which translated as the church), *Seisho no Kenkyu*, no. 119 (10 May 1910), in *Works*, 17:207-8.

The disciples, not learning from Christ, talked about the church too much and brought depravity to it. Because of this we should turn again to Christ on the subject of the church, and ignore the disciples.[9]

3. The Theology of Saint Augustine

Another man who laid the foundation for today's church was Saint Augustine (A.D. 354-430). According to Uchimura, Augustine was a Latin and therefore interpreted the gospel of Christ in a Latin way. The Latins were political people, so Augustine's theology was also political. The doctrine of the so-called original sin came from him, as did the doctrine of atonement. He separated God from man entirely and then tried to harmonize the two by putting Christ between them. Because of this there came to be a great need for the church. The church had to harmonize Christ and the people. Because he was a Latin, Augustine used Christ as an intermediary between God and the people in the same way an intermediary was used between the emperor and his subjects. Uchimura tried to override Augustine: "Do not pay heed to Saint Augustine. Indeed, do not limit yourself to the church's Christianity. Go back to Jesus of Nazareth."[10]

4. Churches in the Early Christian Era

According to Uchimura's study, Christians in the early Christian era did not have a church. They did not have a church building, ministers, bishops, or elders; there was no doctrine or creed. Their *ekklesia* was a church of mere believers alone. Although there is a description of a deaconess at a church in Cenchrea in Romans 16:1, the position of deacon was not the same as it is today. The deacon was, from the very beginning, a caretaker. Uchimura said this verse could rightly be translated as "Phoebe, a caretaker of the church in Cenchrea." It is noteworthy especially that among those Roman Christians Paul named in Romans 16:1-16, not one was invested

9. Uchimura, "Ekurejia," pp. 208-211.
10. Kanzo Uchimura, "Shiso Kondaku no Gensen" (The origin of confusion of thought), *Seisho no Kenkyu*, no. 104 (10 November 1908), in *Works*, 16:82-83.

with the ministry. They did not gather in a church building, as today, but at one of the believers' homes. In other words, a believer's home was a church at that time.

In an article on the church in the early Christian era,[11] Uchimura described the differences between early churches and present-day churches. While he did not deny the existence of churches in the early Christian era, he said that the churches then were fundamentally different from those today. For example, today a church is mainly a place to worship God. The place is called the chapel, and its teacher is usually the officiating priest. The people have prayer, baptism, and the Sacrament, and the Bible is read to them. In other words, today's churches take charge of a believer's religious sentiment. The churches in the early Christian era were not like this. They were societies formed by the believers in an attempt to bring to earth the kingdom of heaven that Christ advocated. Worship, of course, did take place, but it was not everything. Since the church was a society formed by the believers, all things to do with life were addressed in it; namely, bodily matters, their intellect, their food and clothing, their work, their salvation, their education, and other things related to human affairs. The Bible does not mention these matters in detail, but, by putting together random passages, this is certainly the correct conclusion. For example, Acts 2:46 says, "Every day they continued to meet together in the temple courts. They broke bread in their homes and ate together with glad and sincere hearts." "They broke bread in their homes and ate together" does not mean "they held the Sacrament," as some annotators indicate. It means that they ate meals together. It was not the Sacrament, but a banquet. Jesus blessed the daily meals, making them true Lord's Suppers. The Sacrament practiced in churches today was originally the holy feast of the believers, but this pleasant banquet was changed into the formal Sacrament when the heart's love cooled. "The rituals are held when the heart's love grows cold," Uchimura said.[12]

The church, which Christ called "my *ekklesia*," had little chance of becoming depraved. It was a homely gathering with the law of love. "For

11. Kanzo Uchimura, "Shodai no Kyokai wa ikanaru mononarishika" (What kind of church existed in the early Christian era?), *Seisho no Kenkyu*, no. 121 (10 July 1910), in *Works*, 17:276-80.

12. Uchimura, "Shodai no Kyokai wa ikanaru mononarishika," p. 277.

where two or three come together in my name, there am I with them" (Matt. 18:20). In the "church" Christ mentioned here, there would be no room for fighting, jealousy, and luring a person into pitfalls. If a party formed with faith is called a church, a party bound with love is called a home. It is clear that the kingdom of God that Christ mentioned is quite like a home, and bears no resemblance to the church. There were no bishops, elders, and members in the kingdom of God, but father, mother, brothers, and sisters.[13]

> But you are not to be called "Rabbi," for you have only one Master and you are all brothers. And do not call anyone on earth "father," for you have one Father, and he is in heaven. (Matt. 23:8-9)

Despite Christ's clear teachings in the passage above, some came to call the pope papacy (father) and conferred the title of "reverend" on pastors, making the *ekklesia* of love the church of authority. Thus, Christian history was miserable for nineteen hundred years. Indeed, the worst people were the theologians, the products of the church, Uchimura said. Calvin criticized Luther, and both men united and stood against the Roman Catholic Church on the one hand and a group of independent believers called Anabaptists on the other. All this occurred because of the departure from Christ's ideals and the establishment of the earthly church. *Ekklesia* as Christ saw it would be something to love and yearn after.[14]

5. Western Christianity and the Christian Church

Uchimura strongly opposed the idea of "no church, no salvation" that the Western missionaries he had contact with insisted on. In "Kyokai to Kirisuto" (The church and Christ),[15] Uchimura said that, in the West, one who leaves the church loses his faith, and this is obvious to both the person himself and others. This, said Uchimura, was the height of the tragedy. In Western countries Christianity is identical with the Christian

13. Kanzo Uchimura, "Kyokai to Katei" (The church and home), *Seisho no Kenkyu*, no. 123 (10 September 1910), in *Works*, 17:335.

14. Uchimura, "Ekurejia," p. 211.

15. Kanzo Uchimura, "Kyokai to Kirisuto" (The church and Christ), *Seisho no Kenkyu*, no. 132 (10 July 1911), in *Works*, 18:184-90.

church; without the church there is no Christianity. Christianity is always considered the religion the church embraces. Therefore, in the West, those who leave the church certainly cast away their Christian faith, and those who go against the church certainly revolt against Christ. Western believers and nonbelievers alike maintain that there can be no Christianity without the church, and thus many sincere people left the church because they were dissatisfied with it.

Percy Bysshe Shelley (1792-1822), the English poet, was one of them. A man who deeply understood Christ's mind, Shelley publicly called himself an atheist, and English society regarded him as such. Western history has many similar cases. In the United States, Stephen Girard (1750-1831) was called a miser by the church, but he founded a college for male orphans.[16] He was famous for not allowing any church clergy to enter his college premises. In England, Charles Bradlaugh (1833-91) was hated like a viper by the church because he was the leader of atheists. When he was elected to Parliament, the other members excluded him three times on the grounds of his atheism. However, through strenuous effort he not only kept his seat but had a law passed that allowed an atheist member of Parliament like himself not to take an oath in the name of God. An atheist's sincerity was decreed to be sufficient to safeguard his pledge. The man who fought for atheism was a man who had Christ's love, sympathy, and leniency in his heart. On reading Bradlaugh's autobiography, Uchimura thought that if he had been born in England instead of Japan, and had been treated by churches as Bradlaugh was treated, he too would have become an atheist, and would have stood against the church and its Christianity. Other people like Thomas Paine (1737-1809), John Stuart Mill (1806-73), and Herbert Spencer (1820-1903) were all considered atheists, but Uchimura thought they were hardly the enemies of Jesus Christ. Uchimura said that although these people acted contrary to the Christian churches, they were not truly opposed to the teachings of Christ. Further, he said, if there had been no Christian churches, and no doctrine and ecclesiastical authority to compel them, these people would undoubtedly have become Christ's faithful disciples.

Even though the churches have done some good, they turned sincere, benevolent people into atheists. This is the church's irretrievable crime,

16. George P. Rupp, ed., *Semi-Centennial of Girard College* (Philadelphia: Girard College, 1898).

Uchimura said.[17] All this evil arose because the church was associated directly with Christianity. Therefore, in Uchimura's mind the church was not synonymous with Christianity itself.

6. Faith without the Church

The next question is, Can one ever keep his faith if he is distanced from the church? Answering this question, Uchimura said,

> A certain kind of faith cannot be kept at a distance from the church. Certainly, the ecclesiastical faith cannot be kept apart from the church. However, the faith of Christ, which is as it was in the old days, can easily be kept away from the church which is made by men.[18]

If one says he cannot keep his faith without a church, let him look to the Orient, Uchimura said. The Chinese saints still had an influence on the people in the East even without a church to propagate their thoughts. Dante's influence was exerting an effect on the world daily. Christ should be having an even greater influence. If one says a Christian cannot keep his faith without the help of the churches, he is placing Christ below Confucius and Dante, Uchimura said. By trying to protect Christ, the church is instead putting him to shame. Uchimura said, "We certainly can keep our faith in Christ if we distance ourselves from today's church."[19]

In old times the Roman Catholic Church said, "Away from the church, there is no faith. Those who leave the church are abandoned by God." However, brave Martin Luther stood up alone and said, "No, that is not so. There is faith away from the church. God will pick up those who are abandoned by the church."[20] This is how the Protestant churches arose. Today, four hundred years after Luther's death, the Protestant churches that sprang from his work associate the church with the faith, just as the

17. Uchimura, "Kyokai to Kirisuto," pp. 186-87.

18. Kanzo Uchimura, "Kyokai to Shinko" (The church and the faith), *Seisho no Kenkyu*, no. 96 (10 February 1908), in *Works*, 15:386.

19. Uchimura, "Kyokai to Shinko," p. 386.

20. Kanzo Uchimura, "Kyokai to Shinko" (The church and the faith), *Seisho no Kenkyu*, no. 88 (10 June 1907), in *Works*, 15:81-82.

Roman Catholic Church had done. Because of this, Luther has to appear once again, Uchimura said. Indeed, many Luthers have come into the world already. Those who try to take sole possession of God, lose God in the end. The Protestant church today, like the Roman Catholic Church in the old times, recklessly tried to take sole possession of God. Thus the true, living God was lost.

Uchimura said Christ was not the church's exclusive possession. He is possessed by all mankind. As the sun is not the exclusive possession of one country or one particular class, but is for the whole world and all the human race, anybody born as a man has a right to possess Christ as his savior. He does not need to go through the church to be saved. To get sunshine, one does not have to go to a particular place, but needs only to stand under the blue sky, then look up, exposing oneself to the sunshine. In the same way, if one wants to be saved by Christ, one needs only to empty oneself, then look to him, to be saved immediately. Christ, the sun of righteousness, cannot be restricted to a particular church. Like the universe, he is too big. "Anybody who wants to be saved, can be saved directly by him," Uchimura said.[21] Those who seek Christ in the church, or think that one can be saved only through the church, do not recognize Christ as being from God, nor do they recognize him as the savior of the world and the restorer of all things. As Uchimura saw it, Christ had become the captive of the church, in that the church was preventing Christ from being accepted as the savior of all people. By claiming Christ as the church's exclusive possession, the churches at that time were behaving toward Christ as the Pharisees in old times had behaved toward God. "You shut the kingdom of heaven in men's faces. You yourselves do not enter, nor will you let those enter who are trying to" (Matt. 23:13). The church, thinking of Christ as its exclusive possession, can neither come to its own salvation nor bring men to Christ's salvation. Therefore, in order to spread Christ's salvation to all mankind, it is necessary to take Christ out of the church's hands. Releasing Christ from captivity in the church meant that the church that shut off Christ's light was to be removed. Removing the church required people to reach Christ directly without going through the church.[22]

21. Uchimura, "Kyokai to Kirisuto," p. 184.
22. Uchimura, "Kyokai to Kirisuto," p. 185.

7. The Church: Unifier or Divider of Believers?

The clergy always said the church was needed to unite believers. However, as Uchimura saw it, reality was just the opposite. Nothing could prevent the union of believers more than the church. It was estimated that the number of Christian denominations in the world in Uchimura's time was more than six hundred. It was horrifying that the followers of one Lord were split into so many churches, churches that were jealous and hostile toward each other. Not only was there no unity among them, there was competition. Because of this, union of the churches has frequently been urged, both in the West and in Japan. Is it possible for the Christian churches to be united? Can the Anglican Church ever be united with the Methodist church that rose against it? Can the Presbyterian church, which arose from John Calvin's logic, ever be united with the Lutheran church that sprang from Martin Luther's passion? Is it possible that the Anabaptist church, which puts greatest emphasis on the baptismal ceremony, could ever be united with Quakers who see this as unnecessary?

There have been many attempts to unite in the past, but church history clearly shows that every such attempt has ended in failure. Though a lofty ideal may be pursued despite fear of failures, would the union of churches really be ideal? Even if such union were accomplished, it clearly could not be done in less than ten or twenty years and could conceivably only be union among the clergy and not a spiritual union among the believers. Should the disciples of Christ wait for their union for a hundred years while the world is making more rapid progress?

Away from the influence of the churches, Christian union could be accomplished immediately, Uchimura said. Neither God nor the gospel but the man-made churches were preventing it. Thus, by leaving the church, returning to God, and becoming independent, union would be accomplished immediately. The difficulty was not the union of the believers, but the union of the churches. By waiting for the union of the churches, the union of the believers would not be accomplished. It was the church that was preventing the union of the believers. As Thomas Carlyle argued in *Sartor Resartus*,[23] the true union would be accomplished when each one of us becomes an independent man. When a man depends on others, disunion and jealousy are inevitable. Although men differ in

23. Uchimura, "Kyokai to Kirisuto," p. 189.

their occupations, in opinion, in race, and in character, they are neverthe-less all men, Uchimura said. If we want to be united, we must become truly independent men first. By taking the load of the church off our minds and by returning to our true selves, the perfect unity would be accomplished. All unions other than that of true selves would be false unions. Unions of political tactics, therefore, are not the union of God and Christ but are of the devil and politicians. By departing from the church we should be united by the true spirit that God grants each of us through Christ.[24]

8. Does the Church or Faith Come First?

The Roman Catholic Church says the church began with Simon Peter, the son of Jonah, who confessed to Christ, "You are the Christ, the Son of the living God" (Matt. 16:16). Contrary to this, Protestants believe that anybody who has been given a faith identical to Peter's can become the foundation of a church, just as he was. Just as the Roman Catholic Church started with Peter, the Lutheran church started with Luther and the Methodist church with Wesley. Similarly, anyone who embraces the true faith can start a new church. Saying this was neither being haughty nor treacherous, Uchimura argued. It was a fact in religious experience. Uchimura said he advocated his Mukyokai-shugi (Non-churchism) for this reason. Wherever the living Christ is, there is a church, and where the living Christ does not exist, there is no church.

The question, Does the church or faith come first? was an important one. The prosperity of the church cannot be obtained by praying for it. But by praying for the descent of the Holy Spirit on each believer's soul, the prayer is answered and the church then will become prosperous. One does not have to wait for the church to become prosperous. Anyone can make himself the starting point for founding the Kingdom of Heaven, by praying for himself to be the temple of the Holy Spirit. Now is the time in the Christian churches for reconstruction. However, Uchimura thought the church's reconstruction as a church could not be accomplished if the church itself was used as the basis. This was because the church was founded on human faith. Therefore, it must be rebuilt on individuals'

24. Uchimura, "Kyokai to Kirisuto," pp. 187-90.

faith. Some people thought Uchimura was destroying the existing churches, and he argued that in some cases this was so. However, to reconstruct the church properly, some destruction was inevitable. Labor is necessary for the rebirth of the church, and this has taken place many times in the history of the churches, and must take place many more times in the future. Uchimura thought and believed history clearly showed that such labor did not result in destruction, but brought about more solid and sound construction in the church.

9. Modern Churches

Uchimura said those who read the Bible properly would understand that today's church, with its well-appointed building with a piano, an organ, and a pulpit, was not the best place to worship God. Furthermore, today's church had an ambition to increase its influence in the world. According to Uchimura, trying to convert a man to Christianity and making the man a member of the church is making light of God. We can tell people about the gospel, but whether they believe it or not is not up to us, but up to God alone. In addition, true Christians are those who are called by God. Winning people to your side with verbal persuasion is both presumptuous and arrogant and a sin for Christians. There are churches that strive only for the church and do not care for the gospel; the gospel is used by the church to maintain its power. In the same way, a political party strives only for its own party, and forgets the rest of the country. Under these circumstances the country falls victim to the political party, and in the end both the country and the party die. Similarly, the church that strives only for the church will die out, and at the same time belief in the gospel also will decline among the people. A patriot ought not to support a political party that strives only for itself. Likewise, Christians should not associate with a church that cares only for the church, and is enthusiastic only in church affairs but not over Christ. Such churches are delighted to hear of the increase in church members, but are not much pleased to hear of a man who has left sin behind and come to Christ. They do not ask what the truth is, but how good results can be obtained. For them, work is more important than truth, whereas truth should be more important than work. For this reason, what they do is entirely worldly, Uchimura said.

10. The Ecclesiastical Mind

The ecclesiastical mind first forms a party of power, then subjugates the world with it, changing the world into the kingdom of God. That is how the idea of mass politics is applied to religion. The aim is the salvation of people in what the ecclesiastics call the construction of God's kingdom. This is the purpose of the church. The error made by the ecclesiastical mind lies not in its motive, but in the way it is expressed, Uchimura said.[25] Forming a party of power is itself a sign of a worldly mind. Using such a plan, human souls cannot be saved, nor can the kingdom of God be built. For use in God's work, worldly power is rather harmful. Since God humbles the strong and raises up the weak, it would be better not to have it. The idea that if Christians had the majority in parliament this world would change into the kingdom of God is as absurd as the words of the followers of Christ. Because of this, the Roman Catholic Church is fundamentally wrong. Neither do the Protestant churches escape this error. Now, even Mukyokai Christians are likely to extend their influence with this thought in mind. In reality, as a Western proverb says, "Everyone is a Catholic by nature."

Certainly, the ecclesiastical mind is in man's nature. Both church Christians and Mukyokai Christians wish to extend their principles and faith through power. Such thinking also appeared among the apostles when they talked about who was the greatest in the kingdom of God. When Jesus foretold his suffering in Jerusalem, Peter rebuked him and said, "Never, Lord! This shall never happen to you!" But Jesus grew angry and said, "Out of my sight, Satan! You are a stumbling block to me; you do not have the things of God in your mind, but the things of men!" Jesus recognized an ecclesiastical mind in Peter, turning his back to the will of God and obstructing the progress of the gospel. Uchimura said planning prosperity in a church or congregation is equal to destroying the gospel. Just as David in the Old Testament was punished by God for taking a census of the population, we today also incur God's displeasure by using statistics to show the influence of the church. In his article "Kyokai o sakan ni suru Michi" (The way to make the church prosperous), Uchimura wrote,

25. Kanzo Uchimura, "Kyokaiteki Seishin" (The ecclesiastical mind), *Seisho no Kenkyu*, no. 354 (10 January 1930), in *Works*, 32:298-99.

If one wants to make the church prosperous, first he himself must come to know God, and enjoy the power of the faith, and not endeavor to make the church prosperous. Then the church will become prosperous following this. Since the church is different from a political party, and is not the power of this world, it cannot be made prosperous by the means of this world. First, each one of the believers must learn what the Gospel is and then live with it. Then, the church would become prosperous, even if it does not intend to. Understanding simply that Christ is love, and the church, and not seeking the depth, breadth, and height of the love of Christ to its foundation, is not sufficient. Such people achieve nothing, although they have plenty of enthusiasm. As a matter of fact, the church today does not place emphasis on the Gospel of Christ, and for this reason the churches are declining more and more.[26]

One can summarize the differences between Uchimura and the church as he viewed it as follows: (1) The church wanted to have a great influence over the world, bringing it to the kingdom of Christ. Uchimura, on the other hand, was waiting for Christ to descend again from heaven and make this world follow him. (2) The church wanted to have very many members, but Uchimura believed that Christians are always to be small in number to the end of time. (3) The church wanted to convert people into believers, but Uchimura wanted instead to be a witness to the gospel. (4) The church followers wanted to create harmony in this world. Uchimura did not want to make peace with this world, because he knew that this world had been hostile to God from its beginning.[27]

11. Ecclesiastics and Prophets

There have been ecclesiastics throughout all ages: contemptible and incapable politicians who wanted to satisfy their political ambition by commanding and controlling groups of humble believers, because they could not exercise their political ambition openly on the high seas of politics.

26. Kanzo Uchimura, "Kyokai o sakan ni suru Michi" (The way to make the church prosperous), *Dokuritsushinpo*, no. 195 (15 April 1929), in *Works*, 32:98.

27. Kanzo Uchimura, "Kyokai to Yogensha" (Ecclesiastics and prophets), *Seisho no Kenkyu*, no. 152 (10 March 1913), in *Works*, 19:411-13.

The Bible, a blessed gift from God, was turned into a harsh law in the ecclesiastics' hands. They assumed authority, which was, at times, more than an emperor's, claiming that they would govern this world on behalf of God. Because of this the ecclesiastics hated the prophets sent by God. They could not maintain their authority when faced with the truth from the prophets. For example, Amaziah, an ecclesiastic, was against Amos; Pashur, son of Immer, the priest and chief officer in the temple of the Lord, was against Jeremiah. In modern times, Pope Alexander VI was against Savonarola, the patriotic prophet in Florence; Pope Leo X opposed Martin Luther; the Anglican bishop William Laud opposed Oliver Cromwell and John Milton; and Archbishop Poviedonostef of the Russian Orthodox Church opposed Leo Tolstoy. Wherever and whenever a prophet appears, an ecclesiastic comes upon the scene. Satan always disturbs God's works, Uchimura said. The Sadducees who tried and subsequently killed Jesus Christ were the ecclesiastics of that time. Their representative was Caiaphas, the high priest. In Anglican bishop Laud's oppression of the Puritans in England, an ecclesiastic wishing to keep his ecclesiastical authority tried to eliminate God's people. When the glory of the true faith comes to the world, the false believers, the ecclesiastics, raise an uproar. The true enemy of the faith is neither heresy nor heathenism, but the ecclesiastics. There is nothing like an ecclesiastic to do believers harm and corrupt their faith. The church is the fortress where ecclesiastics can shut themselves up.[28]

12. Uchimura's Ideal Church

Uchimura said,

There is a true church. It is Mukyokai (Non-church). It is not a church where a man rules over the others under the system. It is a church where people love, encourage, and help each other through the spirit. Their union and harmony are invisible. Therefore, there is no danger at all of them becoming corrupted. This is the true Holy Catholic church.[29]

28. Uchimura, "Kyokai to Yogensha," p. 413.
29. Kanzo Uchimura, "Makoto no Kyokai" (A true church), *Seisho no Kenkyu*, no. 134 (10 September 1911), in *Works*, 18:258.

What Uchimura was saying here was that true union and harmony exist invisibly. Faith founded on the universe and constructed on earth does not need a church to protect it. If someone asked where the foundation of his faith lay, Uchimura would point to the mountains. If someone asked where his hope for resurrection lay, he would point to the vegetation. Uchimura wrote,

> My God is the one who put the constellation in order. My Savior is the true light which shines on everybody. I do not maintain my faith with the help of theologians. I would make all scientists and philosophers the witnesses of my hope.[30]

Uchimura said,

> There are churches built by bishops and missionaries, but we learn the Bible and want our church built by God. The Bible produced the Lutheran Church in Germany and the Methodist Church in England. Cannot the Bible with the same capability produce the genuine Japanese Church? We can build a solid independent church without asking men's hands.[31]

An independent church is built by independent Christians who depend only on Christ. They need to depend neither on men nor the church. Those who say a man cannot keep his faith without a clergy, or that man's faith grows cold without the church, are not independent believers. The church built by such believers is the church of dependence, though its very name implies independence. Clergy who worry about the faith of believers, and think their faith gets cold unless they are ministered to at the church, have not been brought up in genuine faith. If one saw God in glory even once, he would not easily give up his faith. We must place our faith in the truth itself. The truth takes care of itself. If the truth is taught properly, a follower does not easily give up the faith, as a child does not turn from a good father, even if he is independent from the church and its clergy. Furthermore, Uchimura said that the one who had maintained Christianity in this world for well over nineteen hundred years was neither a

---

30. Kanzo Uchimura, "Kyokai o yoosezaru Shinko" (The faith which does not need the church), *Seisho no Kenkyu*, no. 107 (10 March 1909), in *Works*, 16:241.

31. Kanzo Uchimura, "Dokuritsukyokai no Kensetsu" (The construction of an independent church), *Seisho no Kenkyu*, no. 60 (20 January 1905), in *Works*, 13:6-7.

man nor the church but the Holy Spirit. If God's Holy Spirit had not worked strongly in the believers' hearts, Christianity would have ceased to exist a long time ago. Similarly, the Christian faith has not been sustained in believers by sermons or rites. The reason we have been able to keep our faith until today is that God's Holy Spirit descended on our hearts and filled them, and caused us not to turn from Christ's love, although the devil's forces rose and tried to crush us many times. To think the church was necessary to maintain one's faith makes light of the ability of God's Holy Spirit. If the church is necessary to maintain man's faith, Uchimura asks, "Why do fine churches produce many depraved believers?" Furthermore, if one says that those believers who do not have ministers put themselves in dangerous positions, "Why are there so many degenerate clergies in the world?" "How can those who are not able to maintain their own faith maintain others' faith?"[32]

As "birds of a feather flock together," people with similar faith and discipline naturally gather together and form a party. As a result, a church is unintentionally formed. It is a natural growth, not an artificial work. A true church of God is one that unintentionally becomes a church, led by God's Spirit. The church is not the place where the faith is fostered, but where the faith is confessed and shared with others. We must not go to church to benefit from others, but to do others good and to share good with them. Uchimura repeatedly said, "Since Christians receive a gift of the Spirit directly from Christ the Lord, they do not need to receive it from the church or from the hand of the clergy."[33] Christians build a church to give, and gather there to give. Thus, they do not become dependent on others. However, today's church members have only a mind to receive, not to give.

As we have seen, a Christian was essentially a free man. If a man said he was a Christian but depended on foreign missionaries and the church built by them, this man, Uchimura said, did not yet truly believe in Christ. Uchimura even said, "Independence is the only test of faith for the believers."[34] Those who do not have the spirit of independence certainly do not have the faith. Remarking on the state of Christian churches in Japan,

32. Kanzo Uchimura, "Dokuritsukyokai no Shingi" (The true meaning of the independent church), *Mukyokai*, no. 13 (7 March 1902), in *Works*, 10:62-64.

33. Uchimura, "Dokuritsukyokai no Shingi," p. 64.

34. Uchimura, "Dokuritsukyokai no Shingi," p. 64.

Uchimura said that Japanese Christian churches today were branch offices of European and American churches.[35] Therefore, it was no wonder that they were powerless to save Japanese souls. It was a fact that religion planted by foreign missionaries gradually lost its spirit of independence and became, as it were, the missionary's own possession. He and others had to establish genuine Christianity, given directly by God, among the Japanese.

Uchimura said he was viewed with more suspicion by so-called believers than by unbelievers. The most unfortunate outcome of Uchimura's acceptance of Christianity was that he formed a friendship with church Christians. Now he entered a happy phase of his life by breaking off relations with them completely. An acquaintance of Uchimura and a good Christian once told him that he would never go to Christians to ask for help, even if he was in great trouble, but to unbelievers.[36] Uchimura said he had the same feeling. Fights among believers in the Christian church, especially the severe and offensive fights among the clergy, could not be seen, even in the outside world. What Uchimura saw in the Christian churches in Japan at that time was, he said, worse than the church in Corinth at the time of the apostles. Although crude sins had been committed at Corinth, much deeper and far graver sins were committed in the Japanese churches. Since Christianity was introduced into Japan by foreign missionaries, very strange Christian churches had appeared, Uchimura said. Could they be reformed, or were they even worth reforming? A believer first repents himself, then can guide others to the joy of repentance. In the same way, a Christian church purifies itself first, then can cleanse society. The church was to be an institution to save the world, but the church at that time was not such an institution. The outcry for the reform of the church was the voice of God, and at the same time it was a demand made by both society and the nation. Uchimura said that the churches hated him because he insisted on the reform of the church. He said, "If the church is not able to reform itself, it will die out."[37]

35. Kanzo Uchimura, "Nihon no Kirisutokyokai" (The Christian churches in Japan), *Seisho no Kenkyu*, no. 171 (10 October 1914), in *Works*, 21:107.

36. Kanzo Uchimura, "Yo ga mitaru ima no Kirisutokyokai" (The Christian churches which I observe today), *Seisho no Kenkyu*, no. 93 (10 November 1907), in *Works*, 15:269-71.

37. Kanzo Uchimura, "Kirisutokyokai Kakusei no Hitsuyo" (The need of reform of the Christian circle), *Seisho no Kenkyu*, no. 227 (10 June 1919), in *Works*, 25:41.

Jesus said to them, "The kings of the Gentiles lord it over them; and those who exercise authority over them call themselves Benefactors. But you are not to be like that. Instead, the greatest among you should be like the youngest, and the one who rules like the one who serves." (Luke 22:25-26)

As Jesus says here, a Christian should assume the attitude of a servant toward others, and likewise the Christian church toward other churches. Where there is no such servitude, there is no Christian church. Many Christian churches at that time failed to act in this way. They wanted to rule over the people and the other churches as if they were kings of the Gentiles. Imitating worldly nations, the churches and the ecclesiastics wanted to exercise their authority over other religions and other churches by subjugating them. Their mission work was not service, but a means to expand their influence. The churches at that time were proud of being powerful, and felt ashamed of weakness. They wanted to be the greatest among the people, and not to be their servant. The churches themselves argued, "Who should be the greatest among us?" Therefore, in every respect, the church at that time was not qualified to be called the Christian church. As the church became unworthy of being called a church, believers left it, Uchimura said.[38] Because the churches began to model themselves on the kings of this world, Christ and his true followers left them. However, Christ remained the same and Christians had not died out.

In August 1919 Uchimura wrote a short essay entitled "Sanjozatsuwa" (Miscellaneous talks on a hill).[39] In it he said that the relationship between himself and the church was becoming increasingly estranged. By turning his back on the church, he could enter the unbelievers' world, just as the apostles Paul and Barnabas had done when they said to the Jews, "We now turn to the Gentiles" (Acts 13:46). Uchimura similarly said to the church's clergy, bishops, theologians, and other officials, "We now turn to the unbelievers."[40] He made up his mind never to contend for the reform of the church. Since he loved the church, he advocated its reform, but now he had come to the end of his relationship with it. Therefore he no

38. Kanzo Uchimura, "Kirisutokyokai no Genjo" (The present condition of the Christian churches), *Seisho no Kenkyu*, no. 298 (10 May 1925), in *Works*, 29:98-99.

39. Kanzo Uchimura, "Sanjozatsuwa" (Miscellaneous talks on a hill), *Seisho no Kenkyu*, no. 229 (10 August 1919), in *Works*, 25:98-99.

40. Uchimura, "Sanjozatsuwa," p. 98.

longer needed to advocate its reform. The church theologians said that Uchimura's Christianity would lead the world astray, and would take Christianity along a wrong course. Uchimura said he was very thankful for such criticism. If his Christianity was harmful to the people, he told them not to come to him and believe in him. The relationship between him and the non-Christians was strengthening. He said he now had many friends among Japanese Buddhists. He thought the Japanese were an essentially religious people and not, at least originally, such an atheistic and impious people. The religious nature of the Japanese could not be judged by looking at the Meiji and Taisho periods. Meiji and Taisho society was founded by the politicians from Satsuma and Choshu who were totally insensitive to religion; and it was a most inferior society even in Japanese eyes. There was a time when all Japanese were bonzes. Because the Japanese had such a deeply religious culture over hundreds of years, they were able to reach a glorious position in the world before the World Wars. Uchimura was grateful that such religiousness in Japan had not died out completely. Its forms, Shinto and Buddhism, are different from Western religion, but the deeply religious nature of the Japanese lies concealed at the bottom of their hearts. Uchimura loved this and placed his confidence in this concealed Japan. After leaving the Christian churches in Japan, Uchimura turned to this genuinely religious nature of the Japanese. He said he wished to have friends in faith among the followers of Enshin, Honen, and Shinran, and believed that they would accept the simple gospel of Jesus at last.[41]

13. Uchimura's View of the Church toward the End of His Life

Uchimura spent the latter half of his life as a Mukyokai-shugisha (Non-church Christian), but he loved the Sapporo Independent Church that he and SAC graduates had built, and helped to develop it. From July to September 1928, about two years before his death, Uchimura stayed in Sapporo and helped the Sapporo church, preaching every Sunday. He labored to find a minister for the church, which had none at the time. However, as a Mukyokai-shugisha, helping the church, even the Sapporo

41. Uchimura, "Sanjozatsuwa," pp. 98-99.

Independent Church, was inconsistent with his advocacy of Mukyokai-shugi (Non-churchism). After a minister had been found (Mieji Makino, a follower of Uchimura, became the teacher in charge of the church), Uchimura notified the church in October 1929, a year before his death, that he would resign his position as the adviser to the church, which he had occupied for twelve months. In addition, Uchimura wrote Kingo Miyabe, a member of the church and former SAC classmate, saying,

> I cannot think that the institutional church is the spirit of Christ, therefore supporting of continuity of it prevents the progress of the Gospel. In this point, you and I are of a different opinion beforehand. However, because of the long-time friendship, we saw only each other's virtues, not faults. I have been doing something self-contradictory both to you and to the Sapporo Independent Church. It is inexcusable as a principle, but I excuse it as an affection. Now, at the time of bringing my life work to a conclusion, I must thrust personal considerations aside, then hand down impartial, firm belief to posterity. Thus, I would like to end my life as a genuine Mukyokai-shugisha, cutting off all connection with all institutions which have the name of the church.[42]

Uchimura did not mention in this letter that he was withdrawing his membership from the Sapporo Independent Church; therefore the church treated him as a member until his death in the following year.[43]

42. Uchimura to Miyabe, 14 October 1929, in *Works,* 39:460.
43. Masaike, p. 614.

CHAPTER 6

Uchimura's Mukyokai-shugi

1. Circumstances and Developments in Uchimura's Mukyokai-shugi

Uchimura is known for his insistence on Mukyokai-shugi (Non-church-ism). He started his Christian career with a friendly attitude toward Christian churches and foreign missionaries. In fact, he was baptized at a young age in Sapporo by an American missionary.[1] Uchimura was glad to free himself from traditional Japanese religions, which had a lot of superstitions to bind believers,[2] by converting to Christianity. However, what he found in modern Christianity was that it too was bound, by the institutional church and ecclesiastical authority; and its churches and believers, as he thought, were ruled by the ecclesiastics. Uchimura did not convert to Christianity to be once again bound. Since Christianity, which put emphasis on institutions, was mainly of Western origin, Uchimura started to oppose especially the American and English way of expressing Christianity, and the missionaries who represented these countries. He also developed antichurch, antimissionary feelings during the course of his life because of unhappy experiences with churches[3] and Western missionaries.[4]

---

1. See p. 21.

2. Among traditional Japanese religions, folk religions especially had many superstitions.

3. When Uchimura divorced his first wife, Take, the churches condemned him.

4. When Uchimura was principal at Hokuetsu Gakkan (his first job after returning to Japan from America), he got into serious disagreements with American missionaries at the school over the education of students.

Eventually, in his later years, Uchimura developed Mukyokai-shugi (Non-churchism)[5] and severed completely his connections with institutionalized churches and Western missionaries.

The Mukyokai-shugi that Uchimura advocated was neither no-assembly-ism nor isolationism. What Uchimura wanted in Christianity was freedom. His aim, therefore, was Christianity without any priestly class to officiate. According to Uchimura, faith is given directly from God to each individual. Therefore, there must not be any priest officiating between God and men. One may go directly to the Bible for guidance and consultation without going through the church and its priest or minister. In fact, Uchimura did not recognize any religious authority as a power of this world. What is essential to Christian faith is radical dependence on the gospel, which contains the teachings of Jesus Christ, who taught how to love God and people. Loving God and people was sufficient for Christian faith, Uchimura believed.[6] Things such as baptism, Communion, and other sacraments are not absolutely necessary. He believed that Mukyokai-shugi supported Christ's principles.

Another element that helped Uchimura advocate Mukyokai-shugi was the negative side of existing Christian churches. Uchimura saw in the churches jealousy and hostility among the clergy, mutual exclusiveness, and even conflicts over church membership. In addition, he saw immorality, injustice, insincerity, and distrust among church members. In Uchimura's time, the Western churches and missionaries displayed full power. In this environment, Uchimura was brave enough to stand alone and oppose them. In 1930 Uchimura wrote,

I advocated the Mukyokai-shugi thirty years ago before anybody else advocated it. I did it while the church was not in decline as it is today, and the ministers and missionaries were more powerful than today. At that time, anyone who advocated Mukyokai-shugi was ridiculed, slandered, and treated as a social outcast. By standing up for my principles,

5. Uchimura used the term *Mukyokai* for the first time in 1893, when he was thirty-three. It appeared in his early book *Kirisutoshinto no Nagusame* (The consolations of a Christian). The term *Mukyokai-shugi* appeared, for the first time, in the article "Mukyo-kai-shugi no Zenshin" (The advancement of the Mukyokai-shugi) in *Seisho no Kenkyu* in March 1907.

6. Kanzo Uchimura, "Sekai ni okeru Mukyokai-shugi" (The Mukyokai-shugi of the world), *Seisho no Kenkyu*, no. 113 (10 October 1909), in *Works*, 16:489-90.

naturally then, I could not avoid being lonely. It was indeed a difficult but a happy time. My Mukyokai-shugi was not a principle for the sake of having a principle. It was a principle which, if supported, advanced the faith. It was advocating, as a natural consequence of faith, that "a man is saved not by his actions, but by his faith." Therefore, those who had not had the experience of repenting their sin, could not understand this principle. Only those who had this precious experience accepted it gladly. It was not my principle to attack the church but to advance one's faith. Faith in the crucifixion was paramount and faith in Mukyokai-shugi followed as a natural consequence of this. The crucifixion was of primary importance and Mukyokai-shugi came second or third. I occasionally attacked the church hard because in its faith it had things which did not fit in with the truth of the Gospel. I hated the arrogant and rude Western missionaries, but never hated the church itself. It was clear to everyone that I stood up for the church many times in response to a request while I was advocating Mukyokai-shugi.[7]

2. What Is Mukyokai-shugi?

Mukyokai-shugi, according to Uchimura, does not mean that there should be no churches. It is not an attempt to overthrow anything. Mukyokai (Non-church) is, according to Uchimura, the church for those who have no church.[8] It is like a dormitory for those who have no home. It is also an orphanage or foundling home for the spirit. Uchimura believed there were many Christians without churches in this world. Mukyokai is for them. The true form of the church is Mukyokai, Uchimura said, because there is no organized church in heaven. Bishops, deacons, preachers, and teachers exist only on earth. In heaven, there are neither teachers nor students, neither baptism nor Communion. The Revelation of John says, "I did not see a temple [church] in the city [heaven]" (21:22).[9]

7. This article was found after Uchimura's death and was made public by his surviving family in 1931. The original manuscript is not dated. From its content, however, Norihisa Suzuki thinks it was written by Uchimura in 1930. See *Works*, 32:381.

8. Kanzo Uchimura, "Mukyokai-ron" (An essay on Mukyokai), *Mukyokai*, no. 1 (14 March 1901), in *Works*, 9:71-73.

9. Uchimura, "Mukyokai-ron," pp. 71-73.

3. Christianity and Mukyokai-shugi

Uchimura said that Christianity means living a life with God. Therefore it cannot simply be considered a system or an organization. Life can exist with or without bodily form. "A life" in Hebrew is *ruaḥ,* which can also be translated as "wind" or "breathing," as it is written in the Bible: "The wind blows wherever it pleases. You hear its sound, but you cannot tell where it comes from or where it is going. So it is with everyone born of the Spirit" (John 3:8). Wherever this wind blows, it brings the life of God, and, as the wind leaves no trace of its passing, so the coming of the Holy Spirit leaves no visible sign on believers. Everyone born of the Spirit — that is, all Christians — has a spiritual life. A believer does not have to be a church member. He only needs to be blown by the wind — that is, born of the Spirit. However, since a life, at a certain time, appears in bodily form, it is no wonder that the Spirit of God appears in the form of a church. We should respect such a form, and it is not wrong that we submit ourselves to it on certain occasions. However, when a form (which is a church) becomes more important than God, God acts contrary to it, parts from it, and then abandons it. Mukyokai-shugi is the principle that comes to prominence at such a time.[10]

4. Why Mukyokai-shugi Is Needed

One man may be saved by joining the church, but another may be saved by leaving it. The important thing is to save people. The church is for the people; people do not exist for the church. If a man is saved without the church, Mukyokai is necessary. It is said that God saves the world through the church, but God saves the world through the government as well, Uchimura said. God also saves the world through schools, writing, and art. The ways in which God saves the world are many. Uchimura did not believe that God entrusted the salvation of the world only to the church. "We cannot believe in a God who meets with us only through a certain type of person, the reverends."[11] Mukyokai-shugi is the principle

10. Kanzo Uchimura, "Mukyokai-shugi ni tsuite" (About the Mukyokai-shugi), *Seisho no Kenkyu,* no. 327 (10 October 1927), in *Works,* 30:437-38.

11. Kanzo Uchimura, "Jinrui no Kami" (God for all mankind), *Seisho no Kenkyu,* no. 153 (10 April 1913), in *Works,* 19:439.

that exposes the unnecessary and harmful nature of the worldly system that exists in the name of religion. This principle needs to be continuously exposed until this worldly spirit (the worldly system) becomes completely extinct among so-called Christian churches.[12] Uchimura did not recognize existing religious authority or its influence. He objected to the church because the institution, as a bad system, produced bad men. The fact was, the church served as a hiding place for bad men.

Uchimura did not anticipate that his Mukyokai-shugi would save him. He believed in Mukyokai-shugi because its principle was appealing, suited his character, and deepened his faith. He did not believe everybody had to be a Mukyokai Christian in the same way that he was. In fact, Uchimura did not think the matter of the church was a fundamental question of Christianity. "The church matter is a small thing in one's religious life. It is all right that everyone follows what he chooses in this matter."[13]

5. What Form Should Mukyokai Take, and How Should the Mukyokai Christian Be?

The Mukyokai should willingly form a church, but it should not be a conventional church. It should be a church that is not a church; that is, a spiritual organization that does not need a church building. Uchimura acknowledged that such an organization was inclined to become a conventional church. However, if this became the case, it should be destroyed immediately. The church, like the body of a living thing, degenerates, but is rebuilt continuously. What the church should fear most is anything that might prevent it from evolving. Mukyokai-shugi advocates the destruction of a rigidly defined church and the construction of a living, evolving church. If Mukyokai becomes a conventional, formal church, it should be destroyed by the Mukyokai-shugi.[14]

Mukyokai, even though it does not have any formal organization, nevertheless must not be disorganized. Although Mukyokai Christians make

12. Kanzo Uchimura, "Mukyokai-shugi o sutezu" (Not abandoning the Mukyokai-shugi), *Seisho no Kenkyu*, no. 141 (10 April 1912), in *Works*, 19:90.

13. Kanzo Uchimura, "Mukyokai-shugi no Rigai" (Advantages and disadvantages of Mukyokai-shugi), *Seisho no Kenkyu*, no. 118 (10 April 1910), in *Works*, 17:191.

14. Kanzo Uchimura, "Mukyokai-shugi no Zenshin" (The advancement of the Mukyokai-shugi), *Seisho no Kenkyu*, no. 85 (10 March 1907), in *Works*, 14:489.

light of existing rituals, they should cling to the essence of the gospel. Although they do not associate with the conventional churches, they should show a strong allegiance to the gospel taught to them. After all, Mukyokai Christians should put the New Testament into practice as much as possible.[15]

Mukyokai Christians should not try to force Mukyokai-shugi on the church. That is to say, the Mukyokai Christian should not obstruct the freedom and peace of the conventional church. A Mukyokai Christian should not go to the church and speak for the Mukyokai-shugi. Instead, he should go to the Gentiles as Paul the apostle did. Since there are still millions of Japanese who have not accepted the gospel, there is no need to convert the small number of Christians to Mukyokai. Mukyokai should win genuine unbelievers over to their side. If a Mukyokai Christian is invited to talk at a church, he should talk about the common belief that exists between church Christians and Mukyokai Christians, because there is no difference in the teachings about the love of God between the church and the Mukyokai, the believers and the unbelievers.

6. Other Aspects of Mukyokai

Naturally, as long as we remain on this earth, we need churches. Some people will join churches built by the hands of men, churches of stone or brick or wood. There they will praise God, and there they will hear his word. However, not all of us need churches of this kind. Those who do not belong to organized Christianity need some sort of church while they live on this earth. The church for them is God's universe — nature. Its ceiling is the blue sky, with stars bejeweling its surface; its floor is the green fields and its carpets the multicolored flowers; its musical instruments are pine twigs and its musicians the small birds of the forests; its pulpit is the mountain peaks and its preacher is God himself. This is the church of Mukyokai-shugisha. No church, whether in Rome or in London, can match it. In this sense, Mukyokai has a church. Only those who have no church, in conventional terms, have the true church.[16]

---

15. Uchimura, "Mukyokai-shugi no Zenshin," pp. 489-91.
16. Uchimura, "Mukyokai-ron," p. 73. The translation is largely from *Sources of Japanese Tradition*, vol. 2, compiled by R. Tsunoda, W. T. de Bary, and D. Keene (New York: Columbia University Press, 1958), p. 348.

7. The Leading Figures in the History of Mukyokai Shugisha

According to Uchimura, the ancient prophets in Israel, such as Isaiah and Jeremiah, as well as Elijah and Amos, were Mukyokai-shugisha.[17] Through Elijah, faith in Jehovah, which was about to die out in Israel, was revived and maintained. Amos, the shepherd-prophet of Tekoa, like Elijah, was also a Mukyokai-shugisha. "I was neither a prophet nor a prophet's son, but I was a shepherd, and I also took care of sycamore-fig trees. But the LORD took me from tending the flock and said to me, 'Go, prophesy to my people Israel'" (Amos 7:14-15). Despite objections from the clergy, these men prophesied only because they believed they were called by God to do so. Jesus also was a Mukyokai-shugisha and, because of it, was crucified by Pharisees and Sadducees, the ecclesiastical devotees. Martin Luther was an ardent Mukyokai-shugisha when he proclaimed his new faith for the first time. However, when he founded a church later on he became, according to Uchimura, more of a Pope than the Pope himself. John Milton was a noble, solemn Mukyokai-shugisha all his life, as were Thomas Carlyle, Leo Tolstoy, and Søren Kierkegaard. Uchimura also counted John Wesley, the founder of the Methodist Movement, as a Mukyokai-shugisha. As far as Uchimura knew, the churches that poured both freedom and life into the world, such as the Congregational church, the Baptist church, and others, were started by ardent Mukyokai-shugi. He believed, however, that when a living faith was stiffened, it turned into a church. Therefore, a church was a fossil of faith. What a Christian was supposed to fear most was that his faith might change into a church.[18] In modern times, Kierkegaard (1813-55), a Danish thinker, philosopher, and Christian, brought believers to their senses with his Mukyokai-shugi by delivering a crushing blow to the Lutheran church in northern Europe. Thus Mukyokai-shugi was not a phenomenon unique to modern Japan, Uchimura said. It was a principle that had spread gradually in Western countries ever since Kierkegaard publicly proclaimed his opinions on it.

As to Uchimura's Mukyokai-shugi, the Western missionaries and the church Christians said Mukyokai-shugisha began appearing in Japan only because Uchimura introduced Mukyokai-shugi. Uchimura said this was not true. The truth was that Mukyokai Christians were appearing in Japan

17. Uchimura, "Mukyokai-shugi ni tsuite," pp. 437-38.
18. Uchimura, "Mukyokai-shugi ni tsuite," pp. 437-38.

because there was a need for this faith. God was producing the Mukyokai Christians, and Uchimura believed that he himself had been impelled by God to advocate Mukyokai-shugi. Uchimura said that if he had not upheld this principle, "the stones will cry out" (Luke 19:40). Even if the church, with united efforts, tried to suppress this principle, it would not succeed.[19] Uchimura repeatedly said he had not been the first in world history to enunciate the principle of Mukyokai-shugi. It was supported by Isaiah, Jeremiah, and others, and was still embraced and upheld by many honest Christians today.[20] Further, Uchimura believed that the advancement of humankind and the progress of science were helping this principle. "Those who ridicule Mukyokai-shugi do not understand the general trend of the world," Uchimura said.[21]

8. Establishing a Church on Paper

Uchimura said that the publication *Seisho no Kenkyu*, which became the work of the latter half of his life, was about building a church on paper.[22] This church was not built with wood and stone, nor equipped with a pulpit or seats, but was built on paper. The author of the publication was the pastor, and its readers were the members of the church. It was the simplest and most inexpensive church, yet it would remain after wood, stone, theology, and creed had disappeared. Built on paper, it would last longer than one built with granite. The Christian church was originally such a church, Uchimura said.[23] The Christian church was the book of the Bible before it became the Roman Catholic Church, the Anglican Church, or the Lutheran church. After these man-made churches had fallen down, the church on paper would remain, as the Bible did. God built a permanent church on perishable paper, not with stones and bricks. Because of this, Uchimura would also build his church on paper, so it would remain after all wooden and stone churches fell into ruin.

19. Kanzo Uchimura, "Mukyokai-Shinja no Bokko" (A sudden rise of Mukyokai Christians), *Seisho no Kenkyu*, no. 119 (10 May 1910), in *Works*, 17:213-14.

20. Uchimura, "Mukyokai-shugi o sutezu," pp. 90-93.

21. Uchimura, "Sekai ni okeru Mukyokai-shugi," pp. 489-90.

22. Kanzo Uchimura, "Waga Kyokai" (My church), *Seisho no Kenkyu*, no. 149 (10 December 1912), in *Works*, 19:296.

23. Uchimura, "Waga Kyokai," p. 296.

9. Features of Uchimura's Mukyokai-shugi and the Mukyokai Movement Today

Uchimura's Mukyokai-shugi had, and still has, the following characteristics: (1) It is a Bible-centered form of Christianity. For Uchimura and his followers the Bible was the living word of God. Uchimura himself studied the Bible deeply, prayerfully. (2) It uses the *sensei-deshi* (teacher, rabbi, or master to disciple, follower, or pupil) relationship, traditionally Japanese, to hand on the Christian faith. Today's Mukyokai can be run by choosing one or more leaders from the congregation, not necessarily a *sensei*. (3) There are no ordained clergy or paid ministers in Mukyokai. Uchimura himself was never ordained. It is characteristic of Mukyokai leaders to have another profession and give their Sundays and spare time to evangelism. (4) Everyone going to a Mukyokai service pays an admission fee, usually a specified sum. These fees are usually used to meet the congregation's expenses. (5) Mukyokai, apart from their Bible study groups, have no formal organization whatsoever. There is no local or national Mukyokai organization and no local or national secretary or moderator. (6) Each Mukyokai congregation, following Uchimura's example, publishes its own magazine regularly.[24] (7) Mukyokai's Sunday services, as well as their lectures, Bible classes, discussions, and prayer meetings, are held at private homes or rented halls, since they do not have church buildings.

24. William H. H. Norman, "Non-church Christianity in Japan," *International Review of Missions* 46, no. 184 (1957): 380-93.

CHAPTER 7

Japan: Its Mission to the World

1. Why Japan's Mission to the World?

Uchimura said in his later years that he had formulated three questions from his youth that served as important themes throughout his life. They were: (1) What kind of Christianity would save the human race? (2) How does Christianity relate to Darwinism? (3) What is Japan's mission to the world?[1] Uchimura believed that each country had its own mission to the world given by God, just as each individual has his own mission in this world. In what special field should Japan serve God? What does the world expect from Japan? What should Japan contribute to the progress of mankind? Uchimura said,

> Egypt and Babylonia provided the world with the first material civilization. Phoenicia helped ancient civilization with commerce. Greece produced art, literature, and philosophy, and Judea provided the religion which has not gone out of use until today. A nation has special talent as a country has special products. The human race of the world advances and reaches its ultimate goal by contributions of each country's products and talents.[2]

In what way should the Japanese render service to humankind and to God, and how could they best succeed in doing this?

1. Kanzo Uchimura, *Diary* (2 November 1923), in *Works*, 34:240.
2. Kanzo Uchimura, "Nihon no Tenshoku" (The mission of Japan), *Seisho no Kenkyu*, no. 292 (10 November 1924), in *Works*, 28:400.

2. Japan: An Intermediary between the East and the West

In 1888, when Uchimura was about to leave the United States for Japan, he planned to make a tour of inspection to India and China before reaching his native land. Therefore, he wrote a letter to the president of Amherst College, Julius Seelye, asking his advice on whether he should take this trip. It seems that Seelye told him not to go to India and China, but to go straight back to Japan. From Uchimura's response we know that his ultimate ambition was to Christianize not only Japan but the whole of Asia. He said in his letter,

> I have long been dreaming of visiting India and China for two reasons. First to ascertain the exact position Japan occupies among oriental nations and second, to strengthen my conviction as to the power of Christianity for the heathen, and if the Lord allows, to testify to them what He Himself hath accomplished in my soul. I wish to gather more materials for the solution of great problems which I have had in my mind for many years viz; what shall be the form which Christianity shall assume among the Asiatics, and what responsibilities God hath placed upon the Japanese Christians for the conversions of all Asia.[3]

In another development, in 1894, Uchimura published a book entitled *Chirigakko* (The study of geography).[4] The title of the book was later changed to *Chijinron* (Theory of earth and man). This book investigated each country's mission in relation to its geographical features, and chapter 9, entitled "Nihon no Chiri to sono Tenshoku" (The geography of Japan and its mission), studied Japan's geographical, historical, and ethnological characteristics, and consequently its mission.

In 1849, forty-five years before *Chijinron* was published, Arnold Guyot (1807-84)[5] had published a book with a similar title, *The Earth and Man,* which was, in fact, a series of lectures given at the College of New Jersey (now Princeton University), where he had a teaching position. Uchimura mentioned in his book that he had relied on Guyot's volume for his work.[6] Guyot's

---

3. Uchimura to Seelye, February 1888, in *Works,* 36:280-81.
4. Kanzo Uchimura, *Chirigakko* (The study of geography), in *Works,* 2:352-480.
5. Swiss scholar; professor of physical geography and geology at the College of New Jersey (now Princeton University), from 1854 to 1884.
6. Uchimura, *Chirigakko,* p. 354.

hypothesis was that the world's civilization had been moving westward (he called it "the geographical march of history").[7] He described how the first civilization started in western Asia, in the regions of the Hindu Kush, and Kashmir, then moved to Assyria, Armenia, and Persia. Civilization was next transferred to Greece, to the empire of Alexander, then to the Roman Empire, and later to the other side of the Alps, where its center was established in Germany. Soon thereafter, Europe was entirely civilized. Eventually "the geographical march of civilization" crossed the Atlantic Ocean to America. When Guyot gave his lectures, in the 1840s, the transference from Europe to America was not complete. There were by then many signs of it, however, and Guyot could foretell what would happen in the near future.[8]

When Uchimura read Guyot's book, he probably wondered whether Japan was really destined to join those nations Guyot described. In chapter 9 of his own book Uchimura brought civilization farther west to Japan, where he prophesied the eastward and westward streams of culture would meet and forge a new unity. Then Japan would propagate the new, merged culture to the East and the West.[9] "To reconcile the East with the West; to be the advocate of the East and the harbinger of the West; this we believe to be the mission which Japan is called upon to fulfil."[10] And therefore, Japan's position is similar to that of ancient Greece, which stood between Asia and Europe. Japan will improve what she receives from the West, so that her western neighbors may utilize it and build upon it when the center of historic activity moves farther west.[11]

To further support his idea of Japan as an intermediary between the East and the West, Uchimura compared Japan's geographical features with

7. Arnold Guyot, *The Earth and Man: Lectures on Comparative Physical Geography in Its Relation to the History of Mankind,* trans. C. C. Felton (London: Richard Bentley, 1857), p. 222.

8. Guyot, p. 237.

9. Uchimura, *Chirigakko,* p. 468.

10. Kanzo Uchimura, "Japan's Future as Conceived by a Japanese," *Japan Daily Mail,* 5 February 1892, in *Works,* 1:252.

11. Uchimura, "Japan's Future," pp. 252-53. It is interesting to note that in May 1995, in an interview with the *Financial Times,* a British economic daily, Lee Raymond, the chairman of Exxon, the world's largest oil company, stated, "The centre of our world is moving to the Far East (East Asia)." Reportedly, he cited forecasts that suggest that energy consumption in the region would exceed that of North America or Europe by the year 2005. See David Lascelles, "New Energy for the Fight" (The *FT* Interview: Lee Raymond), *Financial Times* (2 May 1995), p. 18.

those of Britain, which Uchimura also thought an intermediary. In Britain, Uchimura said, the major ports — Glasgow, Liverpool, Bristol, and Queenstown, for example — opened toward North America, while Torquay, Portsmouth, and Southampton were open toward continental Europe. This means that Britain was a go-between for Europe and North America. Britain accepted European civilization, then transmitted it to North America. The reason behind the strength of Britain at that time was that it fulfilled its role of intermediary well.[12] That was Britain's mission. Japan's geographical features similarly demanded that she be an intermediary between North America, which was enjoying the essence of European civilization at that time, and China, which represents Asia. Therefore, Japan's mission was to accept civilization from North America and transmit it to China. Uchimura pointed out that the geographical features of Japan, such as the location of its major ports and mountain ranges, show that Japan was "open" to the Pacific Ocean, the United States, and China, but "closed" to Siberia. The major Japanese ports are concentrated to the Pacific side and to the southwest. Muroran, Matsushima, Yokohama, Shizuoka, and Yokkaichi are on the Pacific Ocean, while Kobe, Fukuoka, Nagasaki, and Sasebo are on southwestern coasts. The Japanese ports facing the Pacific Ocean correspond to North America ports like Vancouver, Seattle, Tacoma, Portland, San Francisco, San Diego, and Acapulco. Also, the Hoang Ho (Yellow River), the Yangtze River, and the Canton River in China flow and open toward Japan.[13] Thus Uchimura claimed that Japan's geographical features and location were inviting her to be an intermediary between North America and Asia.

3. Historical Indications of Japan's Intermediary Role

History also showed that Japan's mission is to be an intermediary between the West and the East. One condition of an intermediary is to be able to understand both sides well. In this respect, Japan was well suited to its role. For example, the Japanese people understood Buddhism. Buddhism had almost disappeared in its native country, India. It went to Mongolia where it turned into Lamaism, an institution that became a superstition,

12. Uchimura, *Chirigakko*, p. 464.
13. Uchimura, *Chirigakko*, pp. 463-64.

controlled by a retired emperor with a Buddhist name. Both in China and Korea, Buddhism occupied a subordinate position to Confucianism, and was believed in only by the lower strata of society. In contrast, in Japan it immediately became the religion of the royal family, which made use of precious articles, the best of the arts, and every possible source of knowledge. Today Japan is the country in the world most affected by Buddha, and the people understand the religion well.

Japan has also been affected by Western civilization. Already heavily influenced by China and India, Japan started absorbing European and American civilization when good contact was made with the West in the mid–nineteenth century. For example, while her western neighbor, China, had not a single foot of railway track, Japan had more than one thousand miles of it. The Peking court had been using the lunar calendar, but Japan used the solar calendar of Newton. In fact, thirty years after Japan opened her door to the world, her people's ability to assimilate different cultures made her into a non-Oriental country. The Japanese accepted Western civilization and assimilated it well, as they had preserved the Oriental civilization and been fostered by it. The Japanese stored Occidental thoughts in their Oriental heads. Thus Japan, understanding both sides of the Pacific, was well suited to be a mediator between the East and the West. For this reason, Japan, standing between democratic, aggressive, and inductive America and imperial, conservative, and deductive China, is in the position "to reconcile the East with the West, to be the advocate of the East and the harbinger of the West; this we believe to be the mission which Japan is called upon to fulfil."[14]

4. Japan's Strong Point: War?

What is Japan's strong point? Some people think it is war. In the past thirty years, Uchimura said in 1924,[15] whenever Japan had been engaged in war, she had won, defeating China and Russia. Many Westerners and many Japanese saw Japan subjugating the world with military power as Assyria and Rome once did. But Japan had only recently been noted as a military power by the world. She had not produced any great conquerors

14. Uchimura, "Japan's Future," p. 252.
15. Uchimura, "Nihon no Tenshoku," p. 401.

such as Alexander the Great and Genghis Khan. The Japanese were brave combatants on the battlefield, but it was not in their nature to like war; they loved peace because the majority were farmers. Although many people have moved out of rural districts, the majority of Japanese still work in agriculture, making this still the foundation of the country.[16] This sort of nation cannot conquer the world with the sword. If one asked the majority of Japanese their view on their lives, they would prefer a peaceful life in a humble cottage as a commoner over being a citizen of a nation that ruled the world. The ideal of the large majority of the Japanese is similar to the ancient Israelites' ideal, expressed by their prophet:

> Never again will there be in it
>   an infant that lives but a few days,
>   or an old man who does not live out his years;
> he who dies at a hundred
>   will be thought a mere youth;
> he who fails to reach a hundred
>   will be considered accursed.
> They will build houses and dwell in them;
>   they will plant vineyards and eat their fruit.
> No longer will they build houses and others live in them,
>   or plant and others eat.
> For as the days of a tree,
>   so will be the days of my people;
> my chosen ones will long enjoy
>   the works of their hands.
> They will not toil in vain
>   or bear children doomed to misfortune;
> for they will be a people blessed by the LORD,
>   they and their descendants with them. (Isa. 65:20-23)

The life of an average Japanese was entirely different from that of Egyptians and Assyrians who relied on war horses and chariots. The main reason the Tokugawa family had ruled Japan peacefully for almost three

---

16. In 1872, over 80 percent of the population was employed in agriculture. This percentage had dropped to 58 percent in 1913 and to less than 50 percent by 1930, although the actual number of people engaged in agriculture has remained more or less constant since 1872. See G. C. Allen, *A Short Economic History of Modern Japan* (London: Macmillan, 1981), p. 250.

hundred years after the unsuccessful attempt to conquer the Asian continent by Hideyoshi Toyotomi (1537-98),[17] was that the Japanese loved
peace.[18] This would also explain why Japan had fewer wars in its history
than the West, Uchimura believed. If a historian were to emerge from
Japan and write a history of the Japanese people, nine-tenths of it would
be the history of peace. Thus, contrary to what modern Japanese history
suggested, winning fame with its military power in the world was not
Japan's mission.

5. A Mercantile Nation?

If Japan is not to become known to the world because of her military
power, should she try to win fame with trade and industry? Uchimura did
not think so. With warships, trade flourishes; with the existence of trade,
industry springs up. A great naval force, great trade, and great industry
were the three foundations on which a so-called powerful nation stands.
Britain was the best example. The Germans fell by trying to model themselves upon Britain, and now the United States of America, also following
the example of Britain, wished to become the world's most powerful
country. By following the example of America and powerful European
nations, Japanese politicians, servicemen, and industrialists were trying to
make Japan one of those great powers; and in fact, this aim had been
accomplished to a certain extent. The question now was whether Japan
could keep its position as a so-called first-class power, obtained by great
effort. By coming to a standstill in every aspect, including politically and
economically, the Japanese were forced to think of "whether so-called
first-class power is the position for Japan to keep." Was it Japan's duty to
enter world competition by having a great naval force, a great merchant
fleet, and trade and industry? Japan was not a country to compete militarily
and economically. She was neither a great military state like Egypt, Assyria,
and old Germany once were, nor a great mercantile nation as Phoenicia,
Venice, and Britain were. Uchimura said there was another way that Japan

17. Feudal lord and the emperor's chief minister (July 1585), completed the sixteenth-
century unification of Japan. He envisaged Japan's domination of the entire East Asia area,
but his death after an unsuccessful invasion of Korea in 1597 caused the seizure of power
by Ieyasu Tokugawa, the first shogun of the Tokugawa shogunate.

18. Uchimura, "Nihon no Tenshoku," p. 402.

could make a great contribution to the progress of the human race, doing the world good and fulfilling her mission.[19]

6. The Japanese: A Spiritual Nation

What is the distinctive feature of the Japanese? Answering this question, Uchimura said the Japanese were a religious nation,[20] as the history of Japan and the nature of the Japanese showed. The people during the Meiji and Taisho periods were not religious; but seventy years, which was the combined span of these two periods, is only a short time in a nation's history. The material civilization of this time was a passing phenomenon. The Meiji and Taisho periods were Japan's childhood. As this time ended the Japanese became aware that by winning fame through military power and through trade and industry, they were going against their nature.

The Japanese were neither tradesmen like the English, nor people who longed for materials like the Americans — they were entirely different people. This was the source of the Japanese people's mission and their greatness, Uchimura believed. Christians in the West might say that Buddhism in Japan today was corrupted superstition, but corruption in Christianity in the West was no different. Sincere, true believers lay concealed in Buddhist circles, just as there were sincere, true believers in the Christian circles in the West. There had been many respectable believers in Buddhist circles in Japan. Uchimura picked out Genshin as a model Buddhist; he could not imagine anyone superior to him among the teachers of religion in all the world, including the West, with regard to purity in faith and loftiness in ideals. In the religious circles of the world, Genshin certainly should be counted among members of the first class, Uchimura said.[21] And other teachers, such as Honen, Nichiren, and Dogen, were all great Buddhists in different sects. Also, in Shinto, Norinaga Motoori and Atsutane Hirata were patriotic believers; they were assets to the country and gave honor to the nation. They all advocated Japan's mission — to guide all nations morally — and called Japan the nation of God in this sense. Their idea of Japan's mission was neither to conquer China and Korea

19. Uchimura, "Nihon no Tenshoku," p. 403.
20. Uchimura, "Nihon no Tenshoku," p. 403.
21. Uchimura, "Nihon no Tenshoku," p. 404.

with military power, nor to extend her influence over the Asian continent, but to shed the light raised in Japan on the darkness of the world. There could be no desires higher, holier, and more patriotic than these. These beliefs dimly reflect the words of Isaiah, the prophet.

> Arise, shine, for your light has come,
>   and the glory of the LORD rises upon you.
> See, darkness covers the earth
>   and thick darkness is over the peoples,
> but the LORD rises upon you
>   and his glory appears over you. (Isa. 60:1-2)

"Darkness covers the earth and thick darkness is over the peoples" was the state of the world in Uchimura's day. The genuine faith could not be found in any country in the world. In Germany, Luther's native country, the faith had changed into the philosophy of religion, or been replaced by social democracy. When one of those attending Uchimura's Christian meeting in Tokyo visited Berlin and introduced to the German Christians what was taught in the congregation in Tokyo, the German Christians were surprised by what they heard. "It is Luther's faith," they said. This meant, Uchimura said, that the German Christians in Luther's native country had forgotten Luther's faith. Similarly the faith of Calvin was rarely seen in Calvin's Switzerland, and conditions in other European countries were nearly the same. Although one might have expected Britain to be the center of Christianity in the world, the British were not the people of faith as expected. The British do not put their trust in uninstitutionalized faith. Therefore, when they leave the church, they almost certainly give up their faith. Moreover, they are exceedingly prejudiced against the mystical. If men like Genshin and Honen appeared in Britain, they would certainly be discounted as dreamers, or as impractical. The faith of Americans was a much more earthly one than that of the British. Their "religion" is perhaps more an enterprise than a religion. They are the people of whom Jesus said, "You would not believe unless you see miraculous signs and wonders." Faith itself is valuable, regardless of its consequence, Uchimura said. It moves God, and overcomes the world.[22]

22. Uchimura, "Nihon no Tenshoku," pp. 405-6.

7. Japan's Mission: Propagation of Christianity in a Pure Form

The world is waiting for the revival of the pure faith once again. So-called Western civilization, at the height of its prosperity, turned out to be the ruin of the world rather than its savior. The United States, reaching the height of material civilization, had a dark future rather than a bright prospect. To the question, How can human happiness be attained? "developing all the material resources of the world" does not seem to be the proper answer. Like a man who has used up most of his life making money and then decided to enter the spiritual world in his old age, mankind is now looking upon the pure faith with longing eyes. Where is this pure faith to be found? Is it not in the Japanese? The Japanese preserved Buddhism after it perished in India, and Confucianism after it declined in China. Again, it might be the Japanese who propagate Christianity, abandoned in America and the European countries, in a new form, after preserving, clarifying, and reviving it.[23]

> Favorable dew dropped on the top of Mount Fuji,
> Trickling, wetting its foot,
> Overflowing, forming two streams to East and West,
> To the West, it crossed the sea,
>   cleansing Chan Bai Mountains,[24]
>   soaking Kunlun Mountains,[25]
>   watering the foot of Tien Shan[26] and Himalaya,
> Arriving at the desert of Judea, it disappeared.
> To the East, it crossed the ocean, putting out the fire of Mammonism
>   at the foot of the Rocky Mountains, cleansing God's altars
>   on the shore of Mississippi and Hudson,
> Flowing into the water of the Atlantic, it disappeared.
> Watching these, the peaks of the Alps rejoiced with singing,
> The Sahara Desert was glad and blossomed like a crocus.
> Thus, the earth was as full of the knowledge of the Lord
>   as the waters cover the sea.
> The kingdom of the world became the Kingdom of Christ.

23. Uchimura, "Nihon no Tenshoku," pp. 406-7.
24. Mountain system on the border between China and Korea.
25. Mountain range between China and India.
26. Mountains in southern Uzbekistan and northern Afghanistan.

Waking up from my dream, I shouted, "Amen, let it be so,
Thy will be done on earth as it is in heaven."[27]

This was the dream Uchimura had, and at the same time, it was the role for Japan he dreamed of. The claim that "Japan is a divine country, and the Japanese a spiritual nation," according to Uchimura, was not mere self-praise. Regarding a sense of honor, and living up to their reputation, the Japanese are first in the world. They must not let their many defects cloud their view of this gift from God. Their ability to keep faith so sensitively may indicate that they are to serve both God and man in the spiritual world. The offspring of Israel, Uchimura argued, were the most influential power in the world of his day, even though their own country no longer existed as a nation.[28] Therefore, the true rise of Japan and the extension of the Japanese influence in the world would come after Japan had given up the position of a so-called first-class world power, though Uchimura did not think that national ruin was always necessary.[29]

Although Japan may have more than one mission, Uchimura believed that propagation of Christianity in its pure form was the most important mission for which Japan was to bear responsibility.

In postwar Japan and today, the existence of deep anti-rearmament feeling among the Japanese is what Uchimura hoped for. On the other hand, today too, in the middle of the 1990s, the fact is that more and more Japanese enterprises are expanding their business and trade, and even causing some trade friction with other countries.[30] This fact arouses one's interest in what Uchimura said about Japan more than sixty years ago. Japan could make a great contribution to the world, but not by becoming a great mercantile nation as Phoenicia, Venice, and Britain once were, though the difference between nineteenth-century British expansion and Japanese expansion today is that the British dominance of trade was supported by British military forces, while Japan today is able to expand without military forces.[31]

27. Kanzo Uchimura, "Hatsuyume" (The first dream of the new year), *Seisho no Kenkyu*, no. 83 (10 January 1907), in *Works*, 14:410-11.

28. The nation of Israel was not founded until 1948.

29. Uchimura, "Nihon no Tenshoku," pp. 407-8.

30. See "Car Wars: Mr Kantor's Outrageous Gamble," *Economist*, 20 May 1995, p. 81 and "Japan Gives Its Answer," *Economist*, 13 May 1995, pp. 79-80.

31. "The Post-Hirohito Century," *Economist*, 17 October 1987, pp. 19-20.

Conclusions

Comparatively little information is available on Kanzo Uchimura in the English language; therefore this study may offer new information to some people. The present writer's intention in this study was to make clear the pattern of receptivity to Christianity in Japan, as documented by Kanzo Uchimura. Originally, the present writer's interest was how an idea or a religion is introduced into a new land and becomes a natural part of the people's lives. In this naturalization process of an idea or a religion, many different phenomena are involved, such as cultural complications, cross-cultural interactions, interpretation, receptivity, and rejection.

In ancient Israel there were two kinds of prophets: (1) institutional prophets who were employed by the rulers (the fact that they were employed by the rulers does not necessarily mean they spoke in their favor; e.g., Isaiah, Jeremiah); (2) prophets who were independent of both the rulers and religious organizations (e.g., Elijah, Amos). The latter group, who spoke out only because they thought they were called by God to do so, condemned and severely criticized religious, social, and political life, religious organizations, and clergy who fell under the authority of the rulers. The independent seers issued warnings to the clergy, the rulers, and society, without the government's guardianship or religious patronage.

In this sense, Uchimura was a prophet of faith and of social righteousness[1] who belonged to this latter group. As a man without power, the

1. William H. H. Norman, "Non-church Christianity in Japan," *International Review of Missions* 46, no. 184 (1957): 382.

government's protection, or the church's patronage, Uchimura criticized the rulers, the churches, and their ecclesiastics and gave warnings to Japanese society. Like the independent prophets in ancient Israel, Uchimura could not avoid the solitude of standing alone, or persecution, or attacks by the church and ecclesiastics. In fact, Uchimura was viewed with suspicion and hostility by both native and foreign Christians. Also, as independent prophets in ancient Israel were never in the mainstream of the religious tradition, so too Uchimura and his followers were never in the mainstream of the Christian tradition in Japan. However, when a country or a society falls into trouble, such prophets come into their own in the same way as independent prophets in ancient Israel delivered their country from national crisis, and revived the faith in Jehovah that had almost died out. During the Second World War, Uchimura's pupils,[2] following in their teacher's antiwar spirit, stood against a Japanese government that was fueling the war effort and turning a blind eye to the Japanese military men who were committing atrocities in East and Southeast Asia. Uchimura's followers were among the very few men of conscience in Japan at that time. However, in postwar Japan, when the values of the Japanese people changed and even national ruin was feared, Shigeru Nambara (1889-1974), Uchimura's pupil and the president of the University of Tokyo, lectured to the public frequently and told the people to take heart and live courageously. The common belief of Uchimura's followers at that time was that Japan's defeat in the Second World War was God's judgment. Therefore, Japan had to be built anew, as their teacher Uchimura had once said: "After this system temporarily ceases to exist, the pure-hearted Japanese who look up to Jesus of Nazareth as the Lord will build a new Japan using more permanent foundations."[3] Thus Uchimura holds a unique place in the Christian circle, and even in Japanese history.

Uchimura was a member of the first generation of Japanese Christians who lived at the time when the country was opened to foreign intercourse, and when Japanese religious ethos was a mixture of Buddhism and Shinto. While the majority of Japanese still placed their faith in scientific learning,

2. Tadao Yanaihara (1893-1961), Hitoshi Masaike (1900-1985), Sukeyoshi Suzuki (1899-1990), and Hyoe Ishihara (1895-1984) were all Uchimura's immediate pupils, and stood up against the war.

3. Kanzo Uchimura, "Shitsubo to Kibo — Nihonkoku no Zento" (Disappointment and hope: The future of Japan), *Seisho no Kenkyu*, no. 33 (10 February 1903), in *Works*, 11:59.

law, and other material things, Uchimura maintained that only true religion would save both the country and individuals. He demonstrated this by disregarding national authority, the emperor, and his potential future success in life. Refusing to bow at the reading of the Imperial Rescript on Education at Daiichi Koto Chugakko in Tokyo in January 1891 was one example of this. Uchimura was a man who suffered for his faith and convictions. Indeed, his religion was a religion of experience. In believing in Christ, he was in danger of losing his life. It is not surprising therefore that such a man found the sectarian, Westernized Christianity, brought to Japan by foreign missionaries, intolerable.

One might say that Uchimura's Christianity was not totally independent of Western influence, because his first contact with the faith came from an American, William S. Clark, who served as an adviser to Sapporo Agricultural College. Also, Uchimura was baptized by an American missionary in Sapporo. Indeed, in the early days of his faith, Uchimura was friendly toward Western Christians and the missionaries who brought Christianity to Japan. As time passed, however, a number of unfortunate incidents occurred between Uchimura and the Western missionaries and churches.[4] Partly because of this he started developing Mukyokai-shugi. Later, many people, including university students, listened to him, and Mukyokai, a pietistic interpretation of Christianity based on the Bible and individual conscience that denied the necessity of clergy or sacraments, was formed. This group was totally independent of any Western Christian denomination — financially as well as theologically. However, Uchimura's Mukyokai-shugi still could not avoid Western Christian influence when it was founded. It could be said that Mukyokai-shugi was the offspring of German Pietism[5] and

4. The clash between Uchimura and American missionaries occurred at Hokuetsugakkan in 1888, over the education of the student. When Uchimura refused to bow at the reading of the Imperial Rescript on Education in 1891 and was subsequently accused of being a traitor to the nation, and when he then allowed a Christian colleague to make a bow on his behalf, the Christian churches, especially the Nihon Kirisuto Kokai (the Church of Christ in Japan), condemned him for his inconsistency. The church also blamed Uchimura when he divorced his first wife, Take.

5. Uchimura said his faith was greatly influenced by Julius H. Seelye, the sixth president of Amherst College in Massachusetts. This has led some to claim Uchimura's faith was influenced by New England Puritanism. Uchimura said, however, that this was wrong. Seelye had embraced a non-American faith, German Pietism, while in Germany as a student. See Kanzo Uchimura, "Kaiko to Zenshin" (Retrospection and advance), *Seisho no Kenkyu*, no. 95 (10 January 1908), in *Works*, 15:373-76.

Quakerism,[6] and also contained Japanese influence.[7]

Uchimura, in spite of his orthodox evangelical beliefs, may not have been spoken of highly in Japanese Christian churches because he advocated Mukyokai-shugi. However, because he introduced Christianity to the Japanese, securing truly Japanese Christianity, he was respected. Uchimura did for Japan what John Knox did for Scotland, Martin Luther for Germany, and John Calvin for France and Switzerland. Conditions in Catholic Europe four hundred years ago were very different from those in non-Christian Japan, so a comparison may be inappropriate. However, when one considers the role Uchimura played, it is apparent that no single man has done as much to present the Christian gospel to the Japanese in a manner suitable for posterity.[8] From 1918 to 1923, in Tokyo, Uchimura preached to between six hundred and eight hundred people every Sunday, the largest congregation in Japan at that time. Uchimura influenced not only Christians in Japan, but non-Christians as well. For example, Uchimura's collected works have been published four times since his death. Many of Uchimura's books, such as *Yo wa ikanishite Kirisutoshinto to narishika* (How I became a Christian: Out of my diary), *Kirisutoshinto no Nagusame* (The consolations of a Christian), *Daihyotekinihonjin* (Japan and the Japanese), and *Denmarukukoku no Hanashi* (The story of Denmark), are still in print and read by both Christian and non-Christian Japanese.

Additional remarks on Uchimura's Mukyokai-shugi should be made here. Uchimura believed that each person could recognize the truth through direct revelation from God. In other words, people do not need any mediator except Jesus Christ. As a natural consequence of this, he opposed any control over people's religious affairs. The Roman Catholic Church claims that only the church and the Pope have the right to interpret the Bible. Uchimura, however, maintained that each individual has this right. Thus, he did not recognize ecclesiastical rulers like ministers, bishops, the Pope, and others, or their authority. Uchimura also believed that true Christians could spread their beliefs without obtaining permission from anybody, just as Jesus Christ had preached the gospel without such

6. Uchimura was influenced by Quakerism while in the United States in the 1880s, especially by Philadelphia Quakers such as Wister and Mary Morris. See Uchimura's letter to Miss Graham, 8 October 1924, in *Works*, 39:176.

7. Uchimura advocated "Christianity grafted onto Bushido." Bushido itself was a traditional Japanese value.

8. Norman, p. 380.

permission. The church insisted that only an ordained person could baptize believers, but Uchimura, as a mere believer, without having been ordained, often baptized small numbers of believers. The church objected to Uchimura's actions, but he did not recognize her authority.[9] Martin Luther advocated "the priesthood of all believers," but he did not put it into practice. In fact, one might say that Uchimura was the one who completed Luther's reformation.[10] Uchimura's congregation had no hierarchy. He also did not call himself a pastor, but always introduced himself as a mere believer. Also, the members of his congregation were completely free to follow their beliefs. For instance, if someone among them did not believe what Uchimura taught, he was not punished. In moral matters, however, those who behaved differently and opposed Uchimura were ordered to leave the congregation. Mukyokai-shugi made use of the *sensei-deshi* (teacher, rabbi, or master to disciple, follower, or pupil) relationship, a typical and traditional Japanese way of handing down ideas and beliefs from one person to another.

Uchimura died in 1930, before the Fifteen Years War, which started with the Manchurian Incident in 1931, the start of Japanese invasion of China, and concluded with Japan's defeat at the end of the Second World War in 1945. However, most of Uchimura's pupils were against Japanese militarism and totalitarianism and were antiwar campaigners during this period. While the majority of Christian churches in Japan supported the Japanese government's war effort, it was mainly members of the Mukyokai, the Holiness Church, and Jehovah's Witnesses who were against the war. These people were therefore persecuted. A considerable number of Mukyokai suffered by losing their jobs,[11] by being examined by the police,[12] and by being imprisoned.[13] In postwar Japan, however, many Mukyokai Chris-

9. Hitoshi Masaike, *Uchimura Kanzo Den* (The Life of Kanzo Uchimura) (Tokyo: Kyobunkan, 1977), p. 330.

10. Masaike, p. 330.

11. Tadao Yanaihara, who became the president of the University of Tokyo in postwar Japan, lost his professor's position in 1937 because of his stand against war. Hitoshi Masaike lost his teaching position at Shizuoka Kotogakko (the Shizuoka Higher School) in 1933 for the same reason, and was arrested in the summer of 1938.

12. The Japanese government found Yushi Itoh (1896-1969) a strong advocate for pacifism through Itoh's magazine *Shin Shion* (New Zion) in November 1937; it placed his magazine under a ban, and arrested him in December 1937.

13. Takeyoshi Fujisawa (1904-1986) founded a Christian magazine, *Kyudo* (Seek after Truth), in 1930. Because Fujisawa's articles on Christian pacifism and criticism of the

tians (especially Uchimura's own pupils) came into prominence. For this reason, the Japanese public turned their attention to Uchimura and Mukyokai. One could even say that postwar Japan was guided by Uchimura's spirit because many important leaders at this time were Uchimura's own pupils.[14]

What, then, was the significance of the Mukyokai Movement when viewed in the context of the world's Christian history? Its import certainly did not lie in the fact that it produced many important leaders in postwar Japan. The present writer tends to agree with Emil Brunner, who defined the significance of the Mukyokai as follows: (1) They are dedicated and radical Protestants following in the spirit of the Reformers; like Luther, they believe in the doctrine of "faith alone" and in "the priesthood of all believers." (2) They train members of their Bible study groups to become independent evangelists. They emphasize the responsibility of every Christian to proclaim the gospel.[15]

Japanese government kept appearing in *Kyudo,* Japanese Special Political Police banned the magazine ten times between October 1933 and August 1937. Finally, in October 1937, they arrested Fujisawa, then imprisoned him.

Sensaku Asami (1868-1952) started a missionary magazine, *Yorokobi no Otozure* (Good News), in July 1931, wherein he advocated an antiwar stance as well as the Christian gospel. Because Asami wrote an antiwar article published in the magazine's October 1937 issue, he was questioned by the police six times, by the military police twice, and by the public prosecutor's office three times; and the magazine was banned. In addition, he was fined fifty yen. In spite of this government oppression, Asami continued his advocacy against war and retained his stance against Japan's national policy, changing the name of his magazine to *Junfukuin* (The Pure Gospel). Finally, the government arrested Asami in July 1943 (at the age of seventy-six), then imprisoned him for more than two hundred days, until February 1944.

Sukeyoshi Suzuki (1899-1990), Uchimura's immediate pupil, was arrested and imprisoned in June 1944 because of his antiwar activities and speeches attacking the government, as Japanese Special Political Police charges specified. He was released in February 1945.

14. Masaike, pp. 5-6. Two postwar presidents of the University of Tokyo (one of the most influential universities in Japan), Shigeru Nambara and Tadao Yanaihara, were Uchimura's immediate pupils. Suke Sakata, president of Kanto Gakuin University in Yokohama, and two chief justices of the Supreme Court in the 1960s and 1970s, Kotaro Tanaka and Masuzo Fujibayashi, were also followers of Uchimura. Tanaka, however, later reconverted to the Roman Catholic faith. At least five ministers of education in postwar cabinets, three prominent scientists, and many men prominent in the arts and professions as well as business also followed Uchimura. Masayoshi Ohira, a former prime minister, claimed to be a Mukyokai Christian, but he was a third-generation Mukyokai.

15. Emil Brunner, "A Unique Christian Mission: The Mukyokai ('Non-church') Movement in Japan," in *Religion and Culture: Essays in Honor of Paul Tillich,* ed. Walter Leibrecht (London: SCM Press, 1959), p. 288.

Mukyokai, apart from their Bible study groups, have no formal organization whatsoever. There is no local or national Mukyokai organization, general secretary, or moderator; no paid or theologically trained ministers and no ordained clergy. Characteristically, many Mukyokai leaders have another profession but devote their Sundays and spare time to evangelism. For this reason, one could say that Mukyokai is a laymen's Bible movement. They want to see a purely lay Christianity, based on the principle of "the priesthood of all believers." Each group usually publishes its own magazine regularly, which fosters communication between groups. Also important here is the annual memorial meeting held in large cities such as Tokyo, Osaka, and Nagoya, near the anniversary of Uchimura's death, March 27. In addition, intergroup Bible study summer camps are held annually at various places, in rotation, where important Mukyokai congregations are located. On these occasions different Mukyokai group members meet each other.

Those who support today's Mukyokai are the third or fourth generation to live since Uchimura. Since Mukyokai neither has a headquarters nor is a federation, there are no statistics available to show how many people consider themselves Mukyokai. However, a rough estimate is that they number, in Japan, from twenty thousand to fifty thousand.[16] Followers of Uchimura's Mukyokai are also to be found today in South Korea and Taiwan.

16. The figure most commonly quoted for the number of Mukyokai followers is fifty thousand. Caldarola gives an estimate of thirty-five thousand, while William H. H. Norman numbers them at twenty thousand. See Carlo Caldarola, *Christianity: The Japanese Way* (Leiden: E. J. Brill, 1979), p. 2; and Norman, pp. 385-86.

Bibliography

I. Works in Japanese

A. Studies of Kanzo Uchimura

Inagaki, Masami. *Uchimura Kanzo no Matsueitachi* (The posterity of Kanzo Uchimura). Tokyo: Asahi Shinbunsha, 1976.

Ishikura, Keiichi, and others, eds. *Uchimura Kanzo Kenkyu* (The Uchimura study). 1973-present.

Masaike, Hitoshi. *Uchimura Kanzo Den* (The life of Kanzo Uchimura). Tokyo: Kyobunkan, 1977.

Ohyama, Tsunao. "Haatofoodo ni okeru Uchimura Kanzo -Kosho-" (Kanzo Uchimura in Hartford — a historical investigation). *Uchimura Study*, no. 10 (April 1978): 75-84.

————. "New England no Uchimura Kanzo" (Kanzo Uchimura in New England). *Geppo* (monthly report), no. 4, p. 4. In *Works*, 1.

B. Works by Kanzo Uchimura

The text used for Uchimura's works is *Uchimura Kanzo Zenshu* (The complete works of Kanzo Uchimura). 40 vols. Tokyo: Iwanami Shoten, 1980-84. References to this collection in the bibliography are indicated by *Works,* followed by the volume number, a colon, and the page number(s).

"Bushido to Kirisutokyo" (Bushido and Christianity). *Seisho no Kenkyu,* no. 186 (10 January 1916). In *Works,* 22:161-62.

"Bushido to Kirisutokyo" (Bushido and Christianity). *Seisho no Kenkyu,* no. 210 (10 January 1918). In *Works,* 24:8.

"Bushido to Kirisutokyo" (Bushido and Christianity). *Seisho no Kenkyu,* no. 339 (10 October 1928). In *Works,* 31:292-97.

Chirigakko (The study of geography). 1894. In *Works,* 2:352-480.

Dendo no Seishin (The Spirit of evangelism). 1894. In *Works,* 2:307-51.

"Dokuritsu Gojunen" (Fifty years of independence). *Seisho no Kenkyu,* no. 335 (10 June 1928). In *Works,* 31:197.

"Dokuritsukirisutokyo ni tsuite" (About independent Christianity). *Yomiuri Shinbun* (Yomiuri Newspaper), 7 June 1925. In *Works,* 29:532-33.

"Dokuritsukyokai no Kensetsu" (The construction of an independent church). *Seisho no Kenkyu,* no. 60 (20 January 1905). In *Works,* 13:6-7.

"Dokuritsukyokai no Shingi" (The true meaning of the independent church). *Mukyokai,* no. 13 (7 March 1902). In *Works,* 10:62-64.

"Ekurejia — Kyokai to yakuserareshi Gengo" (Ekklesia — the original word which translated as the church). *Seisho no Kenkyu,* no. 119 (10 May 1910). In *Works,* 17:204-12.

"Hatsuyume" (The first dream of the new year). *Seisho no Kenkyu,* no. 83 (10 January 1907). In *Works,* 14:410-11.

"Honto no Kyokai" (The true church). *Reiko,* no. 2 (10 November 1921). In *Works,* 26:534-35.

"Ika ni shite Daibungaku o enka" (How can Japan produce good literature?). *Kokumin no Tomo,* nos. 265, 266 (12, 19 October 1895). In *Works,* 3:185-201.

"Jinrui no Kami" (God for all mankind). *Seisho no Kenkyu,* no. 153 (10 April 1913). In *Works,* 19:439.

"Kaiko to Zenshin" (Retrospection and advance). *Seisho no Kenkyu,* no. 95 (10 January 1908). In *Works,* 15:373-76.

"Kami no Nihonkoku" (God's Japan). *Seisho no Kenkyu,* no. 148 (10 November 1912). In *Works,* 19:261.

"Kirisutokyokai Kakusei no Hitsuyo" (The need of reform of the Christian circle). *Seisho no Kenkyu,* no. 227 (10 June 1919). In *Works,* 25:36-41.

"Kirisutokyokai no Genjo" (The present condition of the Christian churches). *Seisho no Kenkyu,* no. 298 (10 May 1925). In *Works,* 29:98-99.

"Kirisutokyosenden to Nihonbunka" (Christian mission and the Japanese culture). *Taiyo* 26, no. 11 (1 October 1920). In *Works,* 25:553-64.

"Kirisutoshinja to Nihonjin" (Christians and the Japanese). *Seisho no Kenkyu*, no. 314 (10 September 1926). In *Works*, 30:59.

Kirisutoshinto no Nagusame (The consolations of a Christian). 1893. In *Works*, 2:3-75.

Kosei e no Saidai Ibutsu (The best memento to posterity). 1897. In *Works*, 4:249-94.

"Kyokai o sakannisuru Michi" (The way to make the church prosperous). *Dokuritsushinpo*, no. 195 (15 April 1929). In *Works*, 32:98.

"Kyokai o yoosezaru Shinko" (The faith which does not need the church). *Seisho no Kenkyu*, no. 107 (10 March 1909). In *Works*, 16:240-41.

"Kyokaiteki Seishin" (The ecclesiastical mind). *Seisho no Kenkyu*, no. 354 (10 January 1930). In *Works*, 32:298-99.

"Kyokai to Fukuin" (The church and the gospel). *Dokuritsushinpo*, no. 200 (15 September 1929). In *Works*, 32:200-202.

"Kyokai to Katei" (The church and home). *Seisho no Kenkyu*, no. 123 (10 September 1910). In *Works*, 17:335.

"Kyokai to Kirisuto" (The church and Christ). *Seisho no Kenkyu*, no. 132 (10 July 1911). In *Works*, 18:184-90.

"Kyokai to Shinko" (The church and the faith). *Seisho no Kenkyo*, no. 96 (10 February 1908). In *Works*, 15:386. Also in no. 88 (10 June 1907); in *Works*, 15:81-82.

"Kyokaisha to Yogensha" (Ecclesiastics and prophets). *Seisho no Kenkyu*, no. 152 (10 March 1913). In *Works*, 19:411-13.

"Makoto no Kyokai" (A true church). *Seisho no Kenkyo*, no. 134 (10 September 1911). In *Works*, 18:258.

"Mukyokai-ron" (An essay on Mukyokai). *Mukyokai*, no. 1 (14 March 1901). In *Works*, 9:71-74.

"Mukyokai-Shinja no Bokko" (A sudden rise of Mukyokai Christians). *Seisho no Kenkyu*, no. 119 (10 May 1910). In *Works*, 17:213-14.

"Mukyokai-shugi ni tsuite" (About the Mukyokai-shugi). *Seisho no Kenkyu*, no. 327 (10 October 1927). In *Works*, 30:437-38.

"Mukyokai-shugi no Rigai" (Advantages and disadvantages of Mukyokai-shugi). *Seisho no Kenkyu*, no. 118 (10 April 1910). In *Works*, 17:191.

"Mukyokai-shugi no Zenshin" (The advancement of the Mukyokai-shugi). *Seisho no Kenkyu*, no. 85 (10 March 1907). In *Works*, 14:489-91.

"Mukyokai-shugi o sutezu" (Not abandoning the Mukyokai-shugi). *Seisho no Kenkyu*, no. 141 (10 April 1912). In *Works*, 19:90-93.

"Nazeni Daibungaku wa idezaruka" (Why does not Japan produce good literature?). *Kokumin no Tomo*, no. 256 (13 July 1895). In *Works*, 3:177-84.

"Nihonkoku no Daikonnan" (Japan's great difficulties). *Seisho no Kenkyu*, no. 35 (10 March 1903). In *Works*, 11:147-56.

"Nihonkoku to Kirisutokyo" (Japan and Christianity). *Seisho no Kenkyu*, no. 301 (10 August 1925). In *Works*, 29:271-78.

"Nihon ni okeru Kirisutokyo no Shorai" (The future of Christianity in Japan). *Seisho no Kenkyu*, no. 135 (10 October 1911). In *Works*, 18:285-86.

"Nihon no Kirisutokyokai" (The Christian churches in Japan). *Seisho no Kenkyu*, no. 171 (10 October 1914). In *Works*, 21:107.

"Nihon no Tenshoku" (The mission of Japan). *Seisho no Kenkyu*, no. 292 (10 November 1924). In *Works*, 28:400-408.

"Nihon o sukuu no Kirisutokyo" (The Christianity which would save Japan). *Tokyo Dokuritsu Zasshi*, no. 30 (5 May 1899). In *Works*, 7:59-60.

"Nihonteki Kirisutokyo" (Japanese Christianity). *Seisho no Kenkyu*, no. 245 (10 December 1920). In *Works*, 25:593.

"Nihon to Kirisutokyo" (Japan and Christianity). *Dokuritsushinpo*, no. 177 (15 October 1927). In *Works*, 30:558-61.

"Niu Ingulando no Uchimura Kanzo" (Kanzo Uchimura in New England). *Geppo* (monthly report) (January 1981). In *Works*, vol. 1.

"Nofu Amos no Kotoba" (Words of the farmer Amos). *Kokumin no Tomo*, no. 253 (13 June 1895). In *Works*, 3:163-71.

"Risoteki Dendoshi" (The ideal evangelist). *Kirisutokyo Shinbun* (Christian Newspaper), nos. 451-55, 18 March–15 April 1892. In *Works*, 1:260-74.

"Sanjozatsuwa" (Miscellaneous talks on a hill). *Seisho no Kenkyu*, no. 229 (10 August 1919). In *Works*, 25:98-99.

"Seishuzakkan" (Miscellaneous thoughts on a fine autumn day). *Seisho no Kenkyu*, no. 230 (10 September 1919). In *Works*, 25:134-35.

"Sekai ni okeru Mukyokai-shugi" (The Mukyokai-shugi of the world). *Seisho no Kenkyu*, no. 113 (10 October 1909). In *Works*, 16:489-90.

"Sekai no Heiwa wa ikanishite kuruka" (How does world peace come?). *Seisho no Kenkyu*, no. 213 (10 April 1918). In *Works*, 24:130-36.

"Senso Haishi Ron" (War-Abolition argument). *Yorozu Choho*, 30 June 1903. In *Works*, 11:296-97.

"Shiso Kondaku no Gensen" (The origin of confusion of thought). *Seisho no Kenkyu*, no. 104 (10 November 1908).

"Shitsubo to Kibo — Nihonkoku no Zento" (Disappointment and hope: The future of Japan). *Seisho no Kenkyu,* no. 33 (10 February 1903). In *Works,* 11:49-59.

"Shodai no Kyokai wa ikanarumono narishika" (What kind of church existed in the early Christian era?). *Seisho no Kenkyu,* no. 121 (10 July 1910). In *Works,* 17:276-80.

"Waga Kyokai" (My church). *Seisho no Kenkyu,* no. 149 (10 December 1912). In *Works,* 19:296.

"Yo ga Hisenronsha to narishi Yurai" (The reasons I became an antiwar protester). *Seisho no Kenkyu,* no. 56 (22 September 1904). In *Works,* 12:423-26.

"Yo ga mitaru ima no Kirisutokyokai" (The Christian churches which I observe today). *Seisho no Kenkyu,* no. 93 (10 November 1907). In *Works,* 15:269-71.

"Yo wa hatashite shinpo shitsutsu aruka" (Is the world making progress?). *Seisho no Kenkyu,* no. 134 (10 September 1911). In *Works,* 18:242-47.

II. Works in Western Languages

Adair, John. *A Life of John Hampden.* London: MacDonald and Jane's, 1976.

Allen, George C. *A Short Economic History of Modern Japan.* London: Macmillan, 1981.

Beasley, W. G. *The Modern History of Japan.* 3d ed. London: Weidenfeld and Nicolson, 1981.

Benedict, Ruth. *The Chrysanthemum and the Sword.* Rutland, Vt.: Charles E. Tuttle, 1974.

Brunner, Emil. "A Unique Christian Mission: The Mukyokai ('Non-church') Movement in Japan." In *Religion and Culture: Essays in Honor of Paul Tillich,* edited by Walter Leibrecht. London: SCM Press, 1959.

Caldarola, Carlo. *Christianity: The Japanese Way.* Leiden: E. J. Brill, 1979.

Carlyle, Thomas. *Selected Writings.* Edited by Alan Shelston. Middlesex: Penguin Books, 1986.

Cary, Otis. *A History of Christianity in Japan.* Rutland, Vt.: Charles E. Tuttle, 1982.

Gosden, Eric. *The Other Ninety-Nine.* London: Marshall, 1982.

Guyot, Arnold. *The Earth and Man: Lectures on Comparative Physical*

Geography, in its Relation to the History of Mankind. Translated by C. C. Felton. London: Richard Bentley, 1857.

Hall, Rachel. *Education in Japan and England: A Personal View.* London: London School of Economics, 1987.

Howes, John F. "Japanese Christian and American Missionaries." In *Changing Japanese Attitudes toward Modernization,* edited by Marius B. Jansen. Princeton, N.J.: Princeton University Press, 1965.

————. "Japan's Enigma: The Young Uchimura Kanzo." Ph.D. diss., Columbia University, 1965.

————. "The Man Kanzo Uchimura." *Japan Studies,* no. 13 (spring 1968). Nishinomiya, Japan: International Institute for Japan Studies, 1968.

Imbrie, William. "The Missionary Message in Relation to Non-Christian Religions." In *Proceedings of the World Missionary Conference in Edinburgh,* pp. 84-85. Edinburgh, Scotland, 1910.

James, Preston E. *All Possible Worlds.* Indianapolis: Odyssey Press, 1977.

Jansen, Marius B. *Japan and Its World.* Princeton, N.J.: Princeton University Press, 1980.

Kraemer, Hendrik. *The Christian Message in a Non-Christian World.* London: Edinburgh House Press, 1938.

Mason, R. H., and J. G. Caiger. *A History of Japan.* New York: Free Press, 1972.

New Encyclopedia Britannica. 30 vols. Chicago: University of Chicago, 1978.

Nish, Ian. *The History of Japan.* London: Faber and Faber, 1968.

Nitobe, Inazo. *Bushido: The Soul of Japan.* 17th ed. Rutland, Vt.: Charles E. Tuttle, 1984.

Norman, William H. H. "Non-church Christianity in Japan." *International Review of Missions* 46, no. 184 (1957): 380-93.

Picken, Stuart D. B. *Christianity and Japan.* Tokyo: Kodansha International, 1983.

Proceedings of the World Missionary Conference in Edinburgh. Edinburgh, Scotland, 1910.

Reischauer, Edwin O. *Japan Past and Present.* London: Gerald Duckworth, 1964.

Rupp, George P., ed. *Semi-Centennial of Girard College.* Philadelphia: Girard College, 1898.

Sansom, George. *A History of Japan: 1615-1867.* London: Cresset Press, 1964.

Sansom, G. B. *The Western World and Japan.* London: Cresset Press, 1965.

Storry, Richard. "History of Japan." In *The Far East and Australasia, 1986.* 17th ed. London: Europa Publications, 1985.

Suzuki, Norihisa. "Christianity." In *Japanese Religion — A Survey by the Agency for Cultural Affairs.* Tokyo: Kodansha International, 1981.

Totman, Conrad. *Japan before Perry — A Short History.* Berkeley, Calif.: University of California Press, 1981.

Tsunoda, R.; de Bary, W. F.; and Keene, D., compilers, "Uchimura Kanzo." In *Sources of Japanese Tradition.* 2 vols. New York: Columbia University Press, 1969-70.

Uchimura, Kanzo. "Again about Sectarianism." *Japan Christian Intelligencer* 2, no. 9 (10 November 1927). In *Works,* 30:477-79.

———. "American Christianity." *Japan Christian Intelligencer* 2, no. 5 (5 July 1927). In *Works,* 30:368.

———. "Americans as Teachers." *Seisho no Kenkyu,* no. 183 (10 October 1915). In *Works,* 21:449.

———. "Bushido and Christianity." *Seisho no Kenkyu,* no. 186 (10 January 1916). In *Works,* 22:161.

———. "Can Americans Teach Japanese in Religion?" *Japan Christian Intelligencer* 1, no. 9 (5 November 1926). In *Works,* 30:98-105.

———. "Christendom versus Heathendom." *Yorozu Choho,* 17 March 1897. In *Works,* 4:59-60.

———. *How I Became a Christian: Out of My Diary.* 1895. In *Works,* 3:1-164.

———. "Japanese Christianity." *Seisho no Kenkyu,* no. 245 (10 December 1920). In *Works,* 25:592.

———. "Japanese Christianity." *Japan Christian Intelligencer* 1, no. 3 (5 May 1926). In *Works,* 29:476-78.

———. "Japan's Future as Conceived by a Japanese." *Japan Daily Mail,* 5 February 1892. In *Works,* 1:243-54.

———. "Justification for the Korean War." *Japan Weekly Mail,* 11 August 1894. In *Works,* 3:38-48.

———. Letter to D. C. Bell, 25 November 1888. In *Works,* 36:305-9.

———. Letter to D. C. Bell, 6 March 1891. In *Works,* 36:331-36.

———. Letter to D. C. Bell, 25 June 1893. In *Works,* 36:378-82.

———. Letter to D. C. Bell, 14 December 1893. In *Works,* 36:385-88.

———. Letter to Julius Seelye, 8 February 1888. In *Works,* 36:275-77.

———. Letter to Kingo Miyabe, 27 October 1884. In *Works,* 36:114-16.

————. Letter to Kingo Miyabe, 27 July 1887. In *Works,* 36:261-63.

————. Letter to Kingo Miyabe, 4 January 1888. In *Works,* 36:272-73.

————. Letter to Kingo Miyabe, 8 January 1891. In *Works,* 36:329-31.

————. Letter to Miss Graham, 8 October 1924. In *Works,* 39:176-77.

————. "Paul a Samurai." *Seisho no Kenkyu,* no. 239 (10 June 1920). In *Works,* 25:362.

————. "To Be Inscribed upon My Tomb." 1886. In *Works,* 40:3.

————. "Two J's." *Japan Christian Intelligencer* 1, no. 7 (9 September 1926). In *Works,* 30:53-54.

Yanaga, Chitoshi. *Japan since Perry.* New York: McGraw-Hill, 1949.

Index